高等职业教育规划教材

空乘服务英语场景会话

English Conversation for Cabin Service

陈 杰　于传奇　编

化学工业出版社

·北京·

内容提要

《空乘服务英语场景会话》遵循高职英语教学的性质和目标要求，以特定行业岗位"空乘服务"为编写内容，结合实际工作场景，注重语言知识技能与行业知识技能的有机结合，符合岗位特色要求。本书以具体任务作为单元编写核心，将行业知识、行业技能、职业行为、情感因素等有机结合起来，注重培养学生的实际能力，提高学生的职业技能。

本教材共分七个单元，基本涵盖空乘服务岗位的主要领域，包括登机、行李安放（Unit 1）；客舱内餐饮服务、商务舱服务、免税商品（Unit 2）；特殊旅客、娱乐、特殊情况（Unit 3）；入境、转机服务（Unit 4）；紧急情况处理、急救（Unit 5）；客舱广播（Unit 6）；知识拓展（Unit 7）。

本书既可作为高职高专、中等专业学校等相关院校空中乘务专业的教学用书，也可作为成人高等教育的同类专业教材，以及作为民航服务人员的参考书及企业培训用书。

图书在版编目（CIP）数据

空乘服务英语场景会话/陈杰，于传奇编．—北京：化学工业出版社，2020.9
高等职业教育规划教材
ISBN 978-7-122-37200-0

Ⅰ．①空… Ⅱ．①陈… ②于… Ⅲ．①民用航空-乘务人员-英语-口语-高等职业教育-教材 Ⅳ．①F560.9

中国版本图书馆CIP数据核字（2020）第098615号

责任编辑：旷英姿　王　可　　　　装帧设计：王晓宇
责任校对：宋　夏

出版发行：化学工业出版社（北京市东城区青年湖南街13号　邮政编码100011）
印　　刷：三河市航远印刷有限公司
装　　订：三河市宇新装订厂
787mm×1092mm　1/16　印张7　字数134千字　2020年9月北京第1版第1次印刷

购书咨询：010-64518888　　　售后服务：010-64518899
网　　址：http://www.cip.com.cn

凡购买本书，如有缺损质量问题，本社销售中心负责调换。

定　价：25.00元　　　　　　　　　　　　　　　　　　　版权所有　违者必究

前言

在航空业日趋国际化的今天，国内外民航业大力发展，航空公司对空中乘务员的要求日益提高，具备良好的乘务英语会话交际能力已是每位空中乘务人员不可或缺的一种职业素质，培养"高素质、严标准、多能力"的乘务员已经越来越成为众多航空公司的共识，且乘务员的英语水平直接决定了其自身的发展空间并影响到良好的航空公司形象的树立。因此，以提高乘务员英语水平为目的的教材相继应运而生。本书基于近年来大量的空中乘务英语教学实践、教学新方法和对新问题的不断摸索，同时结合广大读者的特点和具体需求，以培养职业能力为核心，以工作实践为主线，以学习情境为主体，以乘务工作过程分析为基点编写，以期使读者在了解乘务工作专业知识的背景下，能够熟练掌握并应用英语与客舱乘客友好交流，提供优质的服务。

本书分为七个单元，每一单元由六大部分组成：Word Power（词汇加油站）、Dialogues（对话）、Sentence Patterns（常用句型）、Further Reading（扩展阅读）、Group Practice（小组练习）和Flight Tips（飞行小贴士），其中第六单元与第七单元略有不同。学生需重点掌握客舱对话内容，并能正确使用常用句型，难点在于如何运用所学语言点妥善处理服务中遇到的各种问题。

每一单元都紧密围绕该单元主题设计了重点词汇、客舱对话、常用表达方式、拓展阅读、主题练习以及飞行小贴士六大部分，第六单元与第七单元稍有不同。每一单元主题不同，训练内容也寻求多样化，客舱对话都围绕不同的航线背景展开，强化相关话题和语言功能。在六大部分中，客舱对话和主题练习为编写重点。

本书中的对话内容、常用句型为必须掌握知识，小组练习为实践应用部分，教师应合理利用补充材料和附录部分来组织教学，使学生学会自主学习，并能将知识活用，达到学以致用的目的。本书对业务知识的梳理独具匠心、精心安排；编写思路清晰、结构合理、语言规范；既符合行业规范操作，也适应本专业学生的语言教学要求。

本书由陈杰、于传奇编写，编写过程中得到了很多同事和领导的帮助，深表感谢！由于编者水平有限，加之时间仓促，疏漏和不足之处在所难免，恳请有关专家和读者指正，并提出宝贵意见。

编者

2020年4月

Unit 1　Boarding　登机　　001

1.1　Word Power　词汇加油站 /002

1.2　Dialogues　对话 /002

（1）Welcome Aboard　欢迎登机 /002

（2）Seat Arrangement　安排座位 /003

（3）Baggage Arrangement　安排行李 /005

（4）Pre-takeoff Checking　起飞前检查 /005

1.3　Sentence Patterns　常用句型 /006

1.4　Further Reading　扩展阅读 /007

1.5　Group Practice　小组练习 /010

1.6　Flight Tips　飞行小贴士 /012

Unit 2　In-flight Service　客舱服务　　013

2.1　Word Power　词汇加油站 /014

2.2　Dialogues　对话 /014

（1）Food and Beverage　食品与饮品 /015

（2）Business Class Service　商务舱服务 /015

（3）Duty-free Goods on the Airplane　飞机上的免税品 /016

（4）In-flight Entertainment　机上休闲娱乐 /017

2.3　Sentence Patterns　常用句型 /018

2.4　Further Reading　扩展阅读 /019

2.5　Group Practice　小组练习 /022

2.6　Flight Tips　飞行小贴士 /024

Unit 3 Special Service 特殊服务   025

3.1 Word Power 词汇加油站 /026
3.2 Dialogues 对话 /026
　　（1）Special Meal 特殊餐食 /026
　　（2）Serving a Special Passenger 特殊旅客服务 /027
　　（3）Talking with an Unruly Passenger 与不遵守规定的乘客交谈 /028
　　（4）Turbulence 颠簸 /028
3.3 Sentence Patterns 常用句型 /029
3.4 Further Reading 扩展阅读 /031
3.5 Group Practice 小组练习 /033
3.6 Flight Tips 飞行小贴士 /034

Unit 4 Arrival 到达   035

4.1 Word Power 词汇加油站 /036
4.2 Dialogues 对话 /036
　　（1）Immigration and Customs 移民与海关 /037
　　（2）Introducing a City to a Foreign Passenger 向外国乘客介绍某一城市 /037
　　（3）Flight Transfer 转机 /038
　　（4）Baggage Claim 行李问询 /039
4.3 Sentence Patterns 常用句型 /040
4.4 Further Reading 扩展阅读 /041
4.5 Group Practice 小组练习 /043
4.6 Flight Tips 飞行小贴士 /045

Unit 5 Emergency Handling 紧急情况处理 047

5.1 Word Power 词汇加油站 /048
5.2 Dialogues 对话 /048

（1）Emergency Landing　紧急迫降 /048

　　　（2）Emergency Exits　应急出口 /050

　　　（3）Cabin Decompression　客舱释压 /050

　　　（4）First-aid on Board　机上急救 /051

5.3　Sentence Patterns　常用句型 /053

5.4　Further Reading　扩展阅读 /054

5.5　Group Practice　小组练习 /056

5.6　Flight Tips　飞行小贴士 /058

Unit 6　Cabin Announcements　客舱广播　　061

6.1　Normal Announcements　正常广播 /062

　　　（1）旅客登机时的广播 /062

　　　（2）登机门关闭时的广播 /062

　　　（3）旅客入座后进行客舱设备示范广播（航前安全演示广播）/063

　　　（4）飞机滑行即将起飞的广播 /065

　　　（5）飞机进入平飞阶段的客舱以及航行介绍（起飞后5分钟）/066

　　　（6）供餐前的广播 /066

　　　（7）飞机降落后的广播 /067

　　　（8）旅客下飞机时的广播 /068

6.2　Special Announcements　特殊广播 /069

　　　（1）不同情况下航班延误的广播 /069

　　　（2）飞机遇到颠簸气流的广播 /070

　　　（3）有重病人、备降的广播 /071

　　　（4）遇客舱起火的广播 /071

　　　（5）发生客舱失压的广播 /071

　　　（6）准备紧急迫降的乘务长广播 /072

　　　（7）防止冲击的姿势介绍广播（乘务员规范动作示范）/072

　　　（8）紧急着陆前的广播 /073

　　　（9）延误的广播 /073

Unit 7　Knowledge Extension　知识拓展　　077

7.1　Typical Aircraft　飞机机型 /078
7.2　Famous Airlines　著名航空公司 /084

Appendix 1　附录1 /099
Appendix 2　附录2 /101
Appendix 3　附录3 /103

References　参考文献　　104

Unit 1

Boarding
登机

1.1 Word Power 词汇加油站

WORD and EXPRESSION	MEANING	TYPICAL USE
aisle [əɪl]	n. （座位间的）通道；侧廊	The best seats are in the aisle and as far forward as possible.
overhead locker	行李架	I put it in the overhead locker.
call button	呼唤铃	Please press the call button whenever you need any help.
uneasy [ʌn'i:zi]	adj. 不自在的，心神不安的，不稳定的；不舒服的	She had an uneasy feeling that they were still following her.
cabin ['kæbɪn]	n. 客舱；<美>小木屋	What cabin would you like?
relief [rɪ'li:f]	n. 减轻；安慰；替代	It was unbearably hot, but the cold drinks brought some relief.
stow [stəʊ]	vt. 妥善放置；把……收好	We found seats and stowed our gear.
safety manual	安全手册	There is a safety manual in the pocket.

1.2 Dialogues 对话

（A: Attendant; P: Passenger）

（1）Welcome Aboard 欢迎登机

A: Good morning, sir. Welcome aboard.

P1: Good morning!

A: (To a mother with a baby) Good morning, madam. May I see your boarding card, please? I will show you where your seat is. Please go along the aisle. Your seat is on the right by the window.

P2: Thank you. Where can I put my hand luggage?

A: In the overhead locker, please.

P2: OK, thanks a lot.

A: Under the overhead locker is the call button. If there is anything we can do for you, please press it.

(2) Seat Arrangement 安排座位

(A passenger seems lost in the cabin. A female flight attendant named Laura comes up to him.)

Laura: Morning, sir. Welcome aboard! May I help you?

P1: Morning! Er…, Well, I'm not sure. You see, it's the first time I've flown and I… Well… I'm feeling a bit uneasy about it. Could you show me the way to my seat?

Laura: Oh, I see. Well, there's really nothing to worry about. Could I see your boarding card?

Pl: Um…, oh, yes…, um. Here you are!

Laura: It's 22D in the economy class cabin. Well, it's just in the middle of the cabin, just over there, the aisle seat. This way, please. I'd like to show you your seat.

(When they get there, however, they find that a young lady is sitting in the seat.)

Laura: (to the young lady) Excuse me, madam. May I see your boarding card?

P2: Yes. Here you are!

Laura: Thank you... Madam, I'm afraid you're sitting in the wrong seat. This is 22D, but your seat number is 22K.

P2: Oh, I'm sorry. I thought this was mine. But, where is my seat?

Laura: Let me see, your seat number is 22K. Oh, it's over there, on the right of the cabin. Do you see the window seat next to the exit over there?

P2: Yes, I do. I'll move at once.

Laura: Thank you very much! By the way, the numbers are shown along the edge of the overhead compartment.

P2: OK. Thanks a lot.

Laura: Could I help you carry your bags?

P2: No, thanks. I have one handbag only.

Laura: (to P1) It's OK now, sir. Take your seat, and enjoy your flight.

P2: What a relief! Thank you very much.

Laura: You are welcome.

（3）Baggage Arrangement 安排行李

A: Excuse me, sir. Please put your bagpack in the overhead compartment.

P1: Sure.

A: Excuse me. Is this your bag, sir?

P2: Yes.

A: I'm afraid it's too big to be stowed in the overhead bin. Would you please put it under the seat in front of you?

P2: All right.

A: Thank you, sir.

A: I'm sorry, madam. Please don't put your luggage in the aisle. It will stop passengers trying to pass.

P3: I'm sorry. Just a moment, please. I can't find my shades. I took them off before I got on board and I forgot where I put them.

A: Don't worry, madam. We'll help you find them after all passengers are seated. Please let me help you stow your luggage first.

P3: Thank you.

（4）Pre-takeoff Checking 起飞前检查

A: Excuse me, young lady. Why don't you fasten your seat belt? It's time for us to take off.

P: Er…, but, uh…, I don't like wearing the seat belt, because it makes me feel uncomfortable. If I wear it, I won't feel free at all.

A: But for your safety, your seat belt has to be fastened during take-off and landing and at all times when the seat belt sign is on. You must stay in your seat until this sign is switched off.

P: I'm sorry, I don't know that.

A: Well, there is a safety manual in the pocket. Would you like to go it over with me?

P: Yes. I'd like to.

1.3 Sentence Patterns 常用句型

Expressing Request 表达请求

May I see…?

Could I see…?

Could I help you…?

Would you please…?

Would you like to…?

Offering Help 提供帮助

Is there anything I can do for you?

Can I help you?

Let me give you a hand.

Would you like any help?

If there's anything I can do for you, please let me know.

Don't hesitate to ask me if you have any problems.

The call button and the reading light are above your head. If you need help, don't hesitate to contact me.

Would you like to adjust the air flow?

Expressing and Answering Gratitude 表达与回应感激

Thanks.

Many thanks.

Thanks a lot.

Thank you very much.

I don't know how to thank you.

It's very kind of you to help me.

Thank you for your kindness.

I really appreciate what you have done for me.

1.4 Further Reading 扩展阅读

How to Find the Right Airline Seat

Selecting the right airline can be accomplished completely on the Internet with a little investigation. There is no one size fits all solution when it comes to airline seats, and the informed traveler must make a decision that is appropriate for him after reading advice and suggestions. A good seat can make all the difference in an enjoyable versus extraordinarily uncomfortable trip.

THE ITEMS YOU WILL NEED
① Airline reservation confirmation
② Computer
③ Internet access

STEP 1

Review the airline reservation confirmation to ascertain the type of aircraft operating the flight. Pay close attention to the suffix of the aircraft type, as airlines often operate several variations of the same aircraft. For example, a 737-500 is quite different from a 737-900 in terms of the number of seats, arrangement of seats and locations of exits.

STEP 2

Review the airline's website to confirm the configuration of the aircraft operating the flight. Airlines' websites contain the seating arrangement of each aircraft type in their fleet. And also some relevant Internet sites will provide detailed information regarding each seat on the selected aircraft.

STEP 3

Log into the airline's website, and review the reservation based upon confirmation number and other required personal information. There is usually an option to select seats for the flight.

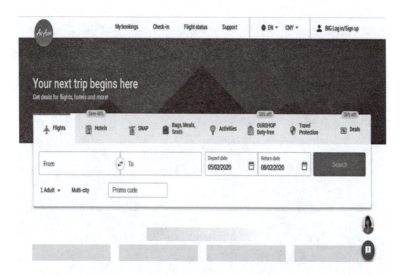

1.5 Group Practice
小组练习

① Look at the following two pictures. What are the people doing? What can they probably say?

② Work with a partner to practice meeting a passenger who doesn't know how to fasten his/her seat belt. Look at the useful expressions in the following box and make up a dialogue to fit your own situation.

> a. I don't know how to fasten my seat belt.
> b. Insert the metal fitting into the buckle.
> c. Pull on the loose end to tighten the belt.
> d. You may do it like this.
> e. Can I unfasten my seat belt now?
> f. When can I unfasten my seat belt?

③ Work with a partner to practice meeting a passenger who is looking for his/her seat. First read the useful expressions above, and then follow the chart to make up a dialogue to fit your own situation.

Greetings and self-introduction

Response

Asking for help: Could you direct me to my seat?

Offering help

Asking if the passenger needs more help

Ending the dialogue

④ Role-play

A. Passengers must be greeted on boarding. It should be cheery and warm but sincere. The attendants stand at each cabin door to welcome the passengers with a smile:

Good morning/afternoon/evening!

Welcome aboard!

B. Ms. Li tries to put her bagpack in the overhead bin. And she needs a CA's help.

C. A mother with a baby enters the cabin with several bags. She leaves her bags in the aisle because her baby is crying; a stewardess goes up to help her.

1.6 Flight Tips
飞行小贴士

Tips to Help You Avoid Jet Lag
助你避免时差反应

① Adjust your bedtime by a hour a day, a few days before your trip.

② Resetting your watch at the beginning of your flight may help you adjust more quickly to the time zone you will be visiting.

③ Drink plenty of water before, during and after your flight.

④ Avoid drinking alcohol or anything with caffeine during your flight.

⑤ Sleep on the plane if it is nighttime at your destination.

⑥ Eat lightly but strategically.

⑦ Relax on the first day at your destination.

Unit 2

In-flight Service
客舱服务

2.1 Word Power 词汇加油站

WORD and EXPRESSION	MEANING	TYPICAL USE
beverage ['bevərɪdʒ]	n. 饮料	And not only food, frequently there must be a beverage.
recommend [ˌrekəˈmend]	vt. 推荐，介绍；劝告	Airlines recommend hard-sided cases for durability.
delicacy [ˈdelɪkəsi]	n. 精美；美味佳肴；敏锐	Both countries are behaving with rare delicacy.
duty-free	免税	Duty-free shops offer a selection of fragrances, liquor, wine, cosmetics, cigarettes, luxury goods and jewelry.
silver [ˈsɪlvə]	n. 银币；银器；银；银灰色 adj. 银的；银色的 vt. 镀银于；使……成银色	She wore a hand-crafted brooch made of silver.
headset [ˈhedset]	n. 戴在头上的耳机或听筒	Soon the wearer of a virtual reality headset will be able to be present at sporting or theatrical events staged thousands of miles away.
adjust [əˈdʒʌst]	vt. 调整，使……适合；校准 vi. 调整，校准；适应	I squinted to adjust my eyes to the dimness.
classical [ˈklæsɪkl]	adj. 古典的；权威的；传统的；正统的	He was a lover of classical music.

2.2 Dialogues 对话

（A: Attendant; P: Passenger）

（1）Food and Beverage 食品与饮品

A: Good afternoon, sir. Would you like something to drink?

P: Yes, please. What have you got?

A: Well, we have coffee, tea, fruit juice, milk, Coca-cola, Sprite, Seven-up, beer and water. Which would you prefer?

P: A cup of coffee, please.

A: How do you like your coffee, with cream or sugar?

P: No, thanks. I'd like to have my coffee black. And make it very strong.

A: And what would you like for the meal? We have chicken, beef, pork and fish.

P: I'm not sure. I'd like to try the beef.

A: OK, here you are, sir. Enjoy it.

P: Oh, it looks nice enough. Thank you.

A: My pleasure.

（2）Business Class Service 商务舱服务

A: Have you decided what you want, sir?

P: Ah, I can't decide right now, actually I'm reading the menu. What do you recommend?

A: For the starter, there's fried calamari and spring rolls, depending on what you like.

P: What are they?

A: Calamari is squid, fried and served with sauce. Spring rolls are wrapped vegetables.

P: I see. I want to try calamari, then.

A: Great! So calamari for the starter. And what about the main course? How would you like the beef? With mushroom sauce?

P: Oh, no beef for me. How is the salmon cooked?

A: It's poached.

P: Hmm…

A: Or why don't you try some fish?

P: I'm afraid not. I'll go with salmon. And for the dessert I'd like chocolate ice cream. By the way, how many meals do you serve on this flight?

A: Two and a half. We'll serve a dinner and a breakfast. In between we'll have some snacks.

P: Sounds good to me!

A: Awesome, we'll bring your starter in an hour. Would you like some more champagne now?

（3）Duty-free Goods on the Airplane　飞机上的免税品

(Announcement: Ladies and gentlemen, we are now selling duty-free goods. You can find the items for sale on the magazine in the pocket in front of you. All the duty-free goods will be at the back of the cabin. We take Visa and Master credit cards only. Thank you!)

P: Hi, I saw this menu. I'm just looking around for something for myself.

A: We have a wide selection of exotic perfume, exciting accessories and cosmetics, all at duty-free prices.

P: The sunglasses look great. Can I take a look at the real things?

A: Sure. Here are the two brands, Dior and Gucci. Which one are you interested in?

P: I have no idea now. Which is better?

A: Let me see what face shape you have. I think you had better try the round and the oval frames, don't you think so?

P: So Gucci is better for me.

A: Any particular color?

P: I'd like to choose the silver one.

A: All right.

(4) In-flight Entertainment 机上休闲娱乐

A: Good afternoon, sir. Can I help you?

P: Afternoon! Please give me a pair of headsets.

A: Here you are, sir.

P: Miss, One of the headsets doesn't work. Could you please change it for me?

A: Yes, of course. Here you are.

P: Can you help me adjust them? I want to listen to some music.

A: Certainly, we have several kinds of music, pop music, classical music and opera. Which type would you like?

P: Maybe I prefer classical music. Which channel is it?

A: The second one. Have you got it?

P: Yes. It's very nice. Thank you for your help.

A: You're welcome.

2.3 Sentence Patterns
常用句型

Expressing Hesitation 表达犹豫不决

I'm not sure…

I can't decide right now.

I'm afraid…

Maybe…

I have no idea.

Showing Likes and Dislikes 表达喜欢和不喜欢

I do like it!

I feel like a glass of beer now.

I adore taking the window seat.

I'd prefer to…

I'm crazy about pop music.

It would be nice to have some.

I can't find the words to express how much I like it.

That's just my cup of tea.

I'm afraid I don't like…

That's not my cup of tea.

There's nothing I like less than it.

I can't stand this kind of music.

Offering Beverage 提供饮品

Would you like something to drink?

What would you like to drink?

Which would you prefer, tea or coffee?

Would you like to have some drinks, sir/madam?

Would you care for some coffee?

What about your preference?

How do you think of Coca-cola?

Giving Advice 提供建议

① Would you like a cup of coffee?

② Would you care for another cup of tea?

③ How about having some fruit juice?

④ Why don't you try this champagne?

⑤ Don't you think it might be a good idea to drink milk?

⑥ I think maybe you ought to have some water.

⑦ Wouldn't you like to have something to drink?

⑧ It might be a good idea to drink some hot drinks.

2.4 Further Reading
扩展阅读

Food Allowance on Airlines

Travelers have always had a love/hate relationship with airplane food. It's not always the tastiest but it fills the need and soothes hunger. However, as cost-cutting measures are causing airlines to phase out free meal service on most domestic flights and passengers are faced with having to pay for sometimes unsatisfying food, it begins to make sense to pack your own tasty treats to eat onboard.

Space Limits

There are officially no restrictions on how much food a passenger can bring onboard. The ever-tightening carry-on regulations mean that you are limited to one small purse or computer bag and one larger carry-on bag that must fit either under your seat in the overhead bin.

Extra Space for Lunch

Pack as much food into a carry-on as desired. Technically there's nothing to stop you from filling an entire carry-on bag with sandwiches, potato chips or chocolate chip cookies, so long as the bag does not exceed the allowed dimensions. Passengers are also allowed to carry on food of a "reasonable amount" to be consumed onboard. In terms of the food that usually translates to an average lunch bag size, enough room for a sandwich, salad and snacks.

Restrictions

Even that lunch bag is subject to the TSA 3-1-1 liquids rules, so keep that in mind when planning onboard meals. Yogurts, hummus, applesauce, soups and even some puddings are considered liquids. According to the TSA, website beverages brought from home are okay if they are in containers of 3.4 ounces or smaller. The same rule applies to canned or jarred sauces, soups, peanut butter, jellies, puddings, Jell-O or other gel-like foods, whipped cream and also cheese spray in pressurized containers. The total amount of these foods in their 3.4-ounce containers must fit in a clear 1-qt. resalable bag to go through security. Foods and beverages in larger containers bought after the security checkpoints are allowed onboard.

Common Courtesy

Other restrictions have more to do with being a good seat neighbor that any legality. If a severely allergic passenger is onboard there could be last minute restrictions on peanut products being brought onto the plane, as those with peanut allergies can experience symptoms even if they're just in the same room with peanuts. Think about odors as you are deciding what to bring for lunch or dinner: the close quarters on a plane make it a less-than-ideal setting for strong smelling foods. Best to leave your Limburger cheese or broccoli at home.

What to Bring

Even with all the restrictions, there are many great options to make your onboard meal tasty and filling. Sandwiches, salads (either pre-dressed or with less than 3 oz. of dressing on the side) and any non-liquid main dish are great to pack. There are no restrictions on fruit, baked goods, chips or candy. If planning to keep food cold to enjoy during a long flight, make sure the ice pack is completely frozen when going through security. Dry ice is also fine as long as it is marked as such and in a vented container.

Clean Your Plate

If flying internationally, remember that there may be restrictions on bringing food off the plane with you. Most countries will not allow fruit or vegetables to be brought in and some countries like Australia don't allow even processed or packaged foods into the country.

2.5 Group Practice
小组练习

① Work with your partner to practice serving a passenger who wants to get something to read. First read the useful expressions in the following, and then make up a dialogue to fit your own situation.

  a. I want to get something to read.
  b. We have newspapers and in-flight magazines. Which one do you prefer?
  c. We have newspapers/magazines in Chinese, English and Japanese.
  d. I want to read some English newspapers.

e. What kinds of newspapers/magazines do you have?

f. You can find newspapers/magazines in front of your seat pocket.

② Look at the following pictures. Try to make up a dialogue about how to select movies on board. Then act it out with your partner.

③ Role-play

A. Ms. Black wants a bloody Mary and soda, but there is no bloody Mary on the airplane. A CA tries to explain this to her, but Ms. Black doesn't seem to understand.

B. The lunchtime has passed, but Ms. Smith is starving. She was sleeping when the CAS were serving the dinner. She presses the call button and a stewardess comes to ask her what she would like to eat.

C. The TV in front of a passenger doesn't seem to work. He intends to turn up the volume but still the voice is too low to be heard. He has to ask a CA for help.

2.6 Flight Tips
飞行小贴士

Cabin Baggage Size
机舱行李尺寸

The carry on or cabin baggage sizes are not standardized. Many airlines base their rules on the guidelines set by IATA (International Air Transport Association). IATA is a group that set up the guidelines for luggage that may be carried. According to IATA rules, the carry on cannot be deeper than 10 inches or 25 centimeters (cm). The maximum length is 22 inches or 56cm and the width is 18 inches or 45cm.

Unit 3

Special Service
特殊服务

3.1 Word Power 词汇加油站

WORD and EXPRESSION	MEANING	TYPICAL USE
vegetarian [ˌvedʒəˈteərɪən]	n. 素食者 adj. 素食的	She is an avowed vegetarian.
marinate [ˈmærɪneɪt]	v. 腌；浸泡	Put it in a screw-top jar with French dressing and leave to marinate.
bumpy [ˈbʌmpi]	adj. 颠簸的；气流不稳的；不平的	We had a bumpy flight over the centre of Panama.
dizzy [ˈdɪzi]	adj. 眩晕的；使人头晕的；愚蠢的	She keeps having dizzy spells.
policy [ˈpɒləsi]	n. 政策；原则；保险单	It is the company policy not to employ smokers.
alcoholic [ˌælkəˈhɒlɪk]	adj. 酒精的，含酒精的 n. 酒鬼，酗酒者	The serving of alcoholic drinks is forbidden.
turbulence [ˈtɜːbjələns]	n. 动荡；骚乱；湍流	Even mild turbulence can shift objects in the overhead bins and send drinks flying off tray tables.
connecting flight	中转航班；转接航班	To which gate do I need to go to catch the connecting flight 707 to New York City?

3.2 Dialogues 对话

（A: Attendant; P: Passenger）

(1) Special Meal　特殊餐食

P: Miss, I can eat none of the food on this menu. I'm a vegetarian. Do you have a special meal for me?

A: Don't worry, just a moment, please. I will check in the galley. We can offer you a vegetarian meal, sir.

P: OK.

A: We have fried noodles with fresh vegetables, marinated vegetables and cut melon. Do you want to try these?

P: Yes, please. By the way, what else can I have?

A: Vegetable hors d'oeuvre or vegetable soup, fruit or bread.

P: The fruit and bread, please.

(2) Serving a Special Passenger 特殊旅客服务

P: Excuse me, Miss. Can you give me a hand?

A: Sure. Are you feeling good? If you are going to sleep, for your safety, fasten your seat belt, please. Our flight could be a little bumpy.

P: I'm not sleeping. I just feel a little dizzy and uncomfortable. Can you bring me some hot water?

A: No problem, sir. Just a moment, please.

P: And an extra sick bag for me, please.

A: Will do, sir.

P: (Suddenly the passenger vomits into a sick bag) I'm sorry for the mess, Miss.

A: Relax, it's nothing serious. Let me help you dump the bag. Do you feel better now? Would you like a cup of hot water?

P: No, don't bother. I feel much better now. I'll just have a good rest.

（3）Talking with an Unruly Passenger
与不遵守规定的乘客交谈

(A passenger already has three glasses of champagne and seeks the attention of a cabin attendant as she is walking past his seat.)

P: Miss. Hurry up, will you? I paid a lot of money for the flight and I want some service.

A: I'm awfully sorry, sir. I am doing the best I can, but you can't drink any more.

P: If you were doing your job properly, you would be able to work out that. I want another glass of champagne.

A: I'm sorry I can't, but I'm happy to help you with something else. I think maybe I could give you a cup of coffee. The coffee on this flight is excellent and I'm sure you would like it.

P: I didn't ask for coffee. I want another drink.

A: We have a policy of serving a maximum of three alcoholic drinks. So I'm sorry, sir. I can't give you any more champagne.

P: Well. I don't want coffee, and I'm not happy. I'll try another airline next time! And I'll write a letter to complain.

（4）Turbulence 颠簸

P: Excuse me, Miss. I wonder whether the turbulence is severe.

A: Don't worry about it. If you feel airsick, you can use the airsickness bag located in the seat pocket in front of you.

P: Oh, I'm OK with the turbulence. I wonder if we'll be late or not; I didn't hear clearly about the announcement just now.

A: We expect to arrive at Beijing Capital International Airport an hour behind the schedule because of the heavy thunderstorm ahead of us. We have to fly around the thunderstorm.

P: I'm afraid I'll miss my connecting flight.

A: It's really a pity, but everything will be all right. If you miss that flight, you can go to the ticket counter and a new arrangement for you will be made.

P: Could you tell me where the ticket counter is?

A: You'll have to go to the domestic terminal after you land. It is just beside the international terminal.

P: Oh, I see. Thank you very much.

A: You are welcome.

3.3 Sentence Patterns 常用句型

Expressing Consolation 表达安慰

Don't worry.

Relax, it's nothing serious.

Don't worry about it.

It's really a pity, but everything will be all right.

Asking for Permission 请求允许

Do you mind if I take it away?

May I have permission to...?

Would you allow me to...?

You don't mind if I put down the shade, do you?

I wonder if I could put the bag on yours.

Would it be possible to exchange your seat with his?

Could you spare me a few minutes?

Are we permitted to fill in the form here?

Is it okay with you if I sit here?

Would it be all right if I put my hand baggage here?

Expressing Happiness and Unhappiness 表达快乐和不快乐

It's a wonderful idea.

Perfect.

That's good to hear it.

It's great to see you again.

That's terrific news.

That's a brilliant idea.

I'm delighted about that.

I'm so proud that you won the game.

It's awful.

Oh God! Things just seem to get worse.

I don't like it. I'd rather…

I can't bear to listen…

I can't stand those rude people.

3.4 Further Reading
扩展阅读

Flying with Children

A recent survey asked travelers if parents or flight crews should be stricter about the behavior of young fliers, including babies, on board. Most emailed stories of kids behaving badly and put the blame on permissive parents. It's true that small children and babies in a cramped cabin can be a nightmare. Here are a few of the responses:

"I've had enough of kids who kicked the back of my seat while their parents looked elsewhere." "It drives me insane to be surrounded by families talking loudly and passing food, drink, toys, clothes, etc., back and forth." Families with kids have every right to fly, but they need to respect my right to a pleasant environment and flight.

The idea of family-only sections on the aircraft was mentioned by many respondents. But families may not enjoy crying babies any more than other passengers. So what is the role of the crew in maintaining security of the plane? A mother and her screaming baby were recently escorted from a plane because the purser considered that other passengers could not

hear the safety instructions announcement. Perhaps that was a little harsh. "It's a delicate situation," one experienced flight attendant says. "If parents can't control their kids, flight attendants have to do what they think is best."

Every situation is different. Cabin crew can ask parents to control their children, but that is often the beginning of "Mind your own business" or "Have you got children?" or "What do you know about kids?" Trying to control another person's misbehaving child can be quite a problem.

"In 15 years, I've never had an unruly child on board who was travelling with a hands-on parent." Airlines sometimes have cards or coloring books to occupy children on board. A few airlines even provide child-friendly tables and chairs and toys at the gate areas to keep small passengers happy before boarding. And one flight attendant was very clear: "Kids are members of the public like everyone else, and they often have to go to places. I'd always prefer to have ten babies on board than one drunk!"

3.5 Group Practice
小组练习

① Make a dialogue on the following situation:

An old passenger is suffering from an earache. You offer him help. However, he refuses and insists that it doesn't matter. So, how can you try to persuade him to accept your help?

② Make up a short conversation according to the given situation:

Tom is a disabled passenger. During the whole flight, a cabin attendant named Lily serves him quite well and helps him a lot. Before disembarkation, Tom sincerely compliments her consideration and kindness.

③ Role play

A. A passenger has air rage. She seems to be irritated at a stewardess and is picking holes in her service. The purser goes to see what is happening and tries to cope with the situation.

B. During the flight a stewardess spills coffee onto a passenger's new and expensive shirt due to a sudden bump during turbulence. The stewardess apologizes to the passenger.

C. A passenger loses one of her contact lenses. She looks for it everywhere but fails to find it. Not knowing what to do, she contacts one of the cabin attendants.

3.6 Flight Tips
飞行小贴士

How to Travel with Your Dog on an Airplane?
怎么样带着宠物狗乘机旅行

Check airlines' pet policies to see if they allow dogs in the cabin or cargo, comparing fees and weight limitations as well as vaccination or health certification requirements. If your dog is able to fly in the cabin, adhere to the dimension limits for under-the-seat carriers. Line with a pee pad and a little blanket such as a baby throw. Make sure your dog's water bottle is empty as you'll have to discard liquids that don't fit TSA guidelines before being screened by security personnel. Make sure your dog is leashed within the carrier because you need to take it out and carry it through the metal detector.

Airlines usually require that you put your pup's carrier under the seat in front of you for takeoff and landing. Whether you can put the carrier on your lap or in the empty seat next to you during the flight depends on the airline's rules, the flight attendants and the reaction of other passengers.

Unit 4

Arrival
到达

4.1 Word Power
词汇加油站

WORD and EXPRESSION	MEANING	TYPICAL USE
complicate ['kɒmplikeit]	v. 使复杂化	Any decision taken by them now, however well meant, could complicate the peace process.
pearl [pɜːl]	n. 珍珠	You do not value what should be valued, so I see I was casting pearls before swine.
souvenir [ˌsuːvəˈnɪə]	n. 纪念品；礼物	He kept a spoon as a souvenir of his journey.
agency [ˈeidʒənsi]	n. 代理机构；服务机构；政府机构	We had to hire maids through an agency.
delay [diˈlei]	n. /v. 延迟；耽搁	The game will be delayed for approximately 30 minutes due to the bad weather condition.
terminal [ˈtɜːminl]	n. 航站楼 adj. 晚期的；末端的	How long does it take to get to the domestic terminal?
carousel [ˌkærəˈsel]	n. 行李传送带	Baggage from Flight AC123 is on the carousel of Number 4.
baggage claim	行李领取	The lost baggage claim counter is for passengers to track and find their lost baggage.

4.2 Dialogues
对话

（A: Attendant; P: Passenger）

（1）Immigration and Customs 移民与海关

P: I wonder if you could help me with this.

A: Certainly. What can I do for you, miss?

P: I'm thinking how I should fill in this Customs Declaration Form. It seems quite complicated, you know, regarding what to be declared and what not to be.

A: Basically everything you bought from abroad should be declared, miss.

P: I know the rules. The truth is that I have a large amount of pearls, but I only paid about ＄50 for them. It's worth at least 3kg of pearls. I'm still not sure if they're real, do I have to declare them, as they're likely fake and I don't want to pay taxes?

A: If you bought 3kg of pearls for $50, they're probably fake. I don't think it's a big deal.

P: I'm still not sure if the Customs officers will "buy my story", as the pearls seem real. If they don't trust me, will I get myself into trouble?

A: Well, I think you should keep two things in mind. First, keep your receipt handy in case they need it any time; second, they may send a specialist to identify your pearls.

P: Okay. I'll take your advice. Thanks for being so helpful.

A: You're welcome. Good luck.

（2）Introducing a City to a Foreign Passenger
向外国乘客介绍某一城市

P: Excuse me, Miss. May I ask a question? Where can I buy a map of Shenyang?

A: You can find the map in any duty-free shop at the airport where we are going to land.

P: Do you know what the local time is?

A: Yes, sir. It's 10 past 4 in the afternoon now. What else can I do for you?

P: I'll be staying in Shenyang for 2 days on a business trip. And possibly I'll have one afternoon and two nights free. Could you recommend me some good places?

A: Sure. The Imperial Palace is an attractive place to many foreigners. During this time of the year they are celebrating the Lantern Festival and there are shows and activities. You can go there in the afternoon. And in the evenings you may go shopping at Zhongjie Street and Taiyuan Street. You will find the goods there at competitive prices. They are the good places for souvenirs.

P: Cool. Are there any English-speaking tour guides if I'd like to visit the Imperial

Palace? Chinese culture is difficult for me to understand, you know.

A: Of course, sir. After you settle at a hotel, you can contact a travel agency, where you can easily find an English-speaking tour guide.

P: I see. Thank you for your help.

（3）Flight Transfer 转机

First officer: Ladies and gentlemen, this is the first officer speaking. Unfortunately I have some bad news for you. The Air Traffic Control has just advised us that, due to a problem on the ground, we need to delay for approximately 30 minutes. I apologize for any inconvenience, and we'll land as soon as possible. In the meantime, please keep your seat belts fastened.

Man: So there is a delay after all. Can we know why?

FA: I'm afraid I can't tell you any more than what the first officer said.

Man: Oh, no, I'm in transit. I've got a connecting flight and do not have much time.

FA: I know. What time is your flight to Munich?

Man: 10:15.

FA: OK. Well, if we land at nine, you'll be OK.

Man: How long does it take to get to the domestic terminal? I've got only hand luggage and I'm checked through, but I do have to clear immigration in Frankfurt, don't I?

FA: Yes, I'm afraid so. It takes about five minutes to get to the terminal. I'm sorry, all what I can say is we'll land as soon as possible.

Man: My God! (Fingers crossed).

(4) Baggage Claim 行李问询

Passenger: Excuse me, Ma'am. My suitcase has never arrived on the carousel. What should I do?

Baggage Agent: You're in the right place. This is the lost luggage claim counter. Let's see if your bag is delayed or missing.

Passenger: I hope it is only delayed. I am here for business and need my suits and the files I've packed in that suitcase.

Baggage Agent: Let's see if we can locate the bag in our system. Perhaps it missed your flight and is on the next flight. The next flight arrives just in sixty minutes.

Passenger: Can you confirm that my suitcase was placed on the next flight?

Baggage Agent: I'm sorry, I can't confirm. Your bag may be missing.

Passenger: What should I do? I have a meeting that starts in two hours!

Baggage Agent: You can go ahead to your hotel. I'll take down your local address. When the bag arrives, an airline service will deliver it to your hotel.

Passenger: I'm staying at the New Continental Hotel downtown.

Baggage Agent: I've added that to our system. Do you have your claim ticket? I need to get your tag number.

Passenger: Yes. When I checked in, they put this sticker on my boarding pass. Is that what you need?

Baggage Agent: Yes, exactly. (Agent types into the computer.) I've keyed your suitcase's tag number into the computer and the search will begin immediately.

Passenger: Do you know when I can expect to receive my bag?

Baggage Agent: I can't give you a firm answer. However, I can tell you that most bags are located within 24 to 48 hours.

Passenger: What if mine isn't?

Baggage Agent: If you don't receive your bag within 24 hours, you should purchase what you need for the next day. Then you can file a claim for those items.

Passenger: And if the bag is lost permanently?

Baggage Agent: You can file a claim for necessary items you bought. Please make sure to fill out this form (hands the passenger a form) and keep all of your receipts.

Passenger: That sure is a lot of work.

Baggage Agent: Don't give up yet. This airport is very large and there are many flights arriving. It is my guess that your suitcase will arrive on another flight this evening.

Passenger: I sure hope so. Thank you for your assistance.

4.3 Sentence Patterns 常用句型

Raising a Problem 提出问题

Something is missing/broken/not working.

There's a problem.

I am afraid I can not...

There's something wrong with it.

What should I do?

What if...

Expressing "I understand" 表达"我理解"

I fully understand you.

I see.

It's not hard to understand.

It's quite comprehensible.

If I were you, I would think exactly the same.

That's not rocket science.

That's understandable.

Expressing Wishes 表达愿望

Best wishes to you.

May I wish you every success for the future?

I wish you good health.

I wish you a happy new year.

Many happy returns (of the day)!

Have a pleasant journey.

Best wishes for a speedy recovery.

I hope you have a good time.

Wish you good health and lots of happiness.

Expressing Instructions 指示说明

First of all, you should remember to do that.

You should arrange your luggage when you first get on board.

The following procedure should be adopted.

Look, all you have to do is…

You can do it like this: press the button and lean back at the same time.

Let me show you, First…Then… After that… And finally… Have you got it?

After you've done that, you…

The next thing you should do is…

The last thing you should do is…

4.4 Further Reading
扩展阅读

Singapore Changi Airport

Shop, dine and relax at the world's most awarded airport. Beauty products. Electronics.

Designer brands. Souvenirs. International cuisine. Authentic local fare. With over 500 retail and dining outlets across four world-class terminals and Jewel, there's bound to be something for you whether you're transiting, departing from, or arriving at Singapore Changi Airport.

When you arrive at Changi Airport, check the flight information displayed for the departure terminal and the gate of your connecting flight. Or, you can approach the Transfer Desk staff for assistance. Do note that Changi Airport does not broadcast final call or name paging announcements.

During your transit, you can enjoy a host of comforts and conveniences such as free WiFi and entertainment at Changi Airport. If you have at least five hours before your connecting flight and the necessary travel documents to enter Singapore, you can visit Jewel, a retail and lifestyle complex that's directly connected to Terminal 1 Arrival Hall, and a link bridge (5-10 minute walk) away from Terminal 2 and 3.

Free Internet connectivity across all four terminals for your laptops and mobile devices, or surf at any of the 400 free Internet kiosks. More than 800 free charging points for your electronic devices.

It's fun for kids with playgrounds and activity stations! For travelers with young children, the convenient Baby Care Rooms offer privacy for mums of infants, as well as a hot water dispenser.

Catch a movie at 24-hour movie theaters in Terminal 2 and 3. Gamers can pass the time quickly with free LAN gaming at the Entertainment Deck in Terminal 2.

Relax with full body massages, manicure/pedicure treatments or even a haircut at the Ambassador Transit Lounges or Plaza Premium Lounge. Equipped with gym and shower facilities, these pay-per-use lounges are popular with passengers who wish to freshen up while on transit. Free foot massage machines are also available across all terminals.

At 40m high, the HSBC Rain Vortex is a majestic sight at the heart of Jewel Changi Airport. Visit there when night falls for a memorizing light and sound show.

Follow the Shiseido Forest Valley walking trails in Jewel Changi Airport to immerse yourself in four fascinating storeys of shrubs, trees and other lush greenery.

With plenty of dining options that open past midnight in Jewel Changi Airport, you won't have to compromise on food —— even if you're arriving late.

4.5 Group Practice 小组练习

① What should the safety check crew conduct before arrival? Make a checklist together with your group members.

> Cabin safety checklist
> - Tray table folded
> - Armrest lowered
> - ....

- ....
- ....
- ....
- ....
- ....
- ....
- ....
- ....

② Work with a partner. Which of these sentences should the crew use during the last 20 minutes of the flight, and which during the last ten minutes before arrival?

1. Have you filled in your disembarkation card, sir?

2. Any rubbish?

3. I'm sorry, you'll have to wait until we land, sir.

4. Could you put your seat upright, please, sir?

5. Could you remove your headset, please, madam?

6. I'm afraid the toilet is now locked for landing, madam.

7. This is the emergency exit door, sir. You'll have to put your bag in the overhead locker.

8. I'm sorry, it's too late now, madam.

9. Please, sir, I've required you before, you must switch off your laptop immediately.

10. Could you fasten your child's seatbelt, please, sir?

11. Could you just open the window blind? Thanks.

12. Yes, but not now – I'll tell you after landing.

③ Work with a partner. Discuss these questions.

Ⅰ. Do you agree that preparing for landing is the most stressful part of the flight? If so, why?

Ⅱ. On long-haul flights, why doesn't the captain announce the beginning of the descent at least 30 minutes before landing, to give cabin crew more time to perform all their duties? On short-haul flights, is 20 minutes enough for the cabin crew?

Ⅲ. Can you suggest improvements to the communications between the flight crew and the cabin crew during the last ten minutes before landing?

Ⅳ. How do you deal with the passengers who ask for information about baggage, transit, how to get into town and so on when you are preparing for landing?

4.6 Flight Tips
飞行小贴士

What do the flight attendants do after passenger disembark?
乘客下机后空乘的工作就结束了吗？听听现役空乘怎么说

"When we're on the ground, we check the aircraft in case anything has been left behind. It's amazing what we find —— valuables, passports, immigration forms. Once I found a wallet full of money! I took it to the 'Lost and Found' counter. Fortunately, I met the passenger who had lost it. He explained that the money was for tuition fees and six months' living expenses. I can't believe he would forget something like that! I've found other strange things, too. I once found a diamond ring in the lavatory and a wig in an overhead locker. One lady even left her false teeth on her lunch tray and we had to search through all the rubbish to find them! At the end of a flight you should make sure:

- every passenger leaves the plane safely with all their hand luggage.
- complete a written flight report and record any unusual incidents.
- add up and record all food and drink orders and duty-free sales.

When all the hard work is done. You can check into your hotel, relax, and explore the destination before your next flight!"

——*Emirates Crew*

Unit 5

Emergency Handling
紧急情况处理

5.1 Word Power 词汇加油站

WORD and EXPRESSION	MEANING	TYPICAL USE
emergency [i'mɜːdʒənsi]	n. 紧急情况；突发事件	Emergency exits are clearly marked on both sides of the aircraft.
instruction [in'strʌkʃn]	n. 指令，指示	Please listen to the crew's instructions carefully.
descend [di'send]	v. 下来，下降	Please keep your masks on while we descend to a lower altitude.
announcement [ə'naʊnsmənt]	n. 公告，通告	I think we need a doctor. Can you make an announcement immediately?
bracing position	防撞击姿势	It also shows the bracing position, which you must adopt while an emergency landing.
safety procedure	安全规程	We are going to take you through our safety procedures.
on medication	在进行药物治疗中	He's a diabetic and has been on medication for many years.

5.2 Dialogues 对话

(C: Captain; M: Flight Service Manager; A: Fight Attendant; P: Passenger; D: Doctor; W: Wife)

（1）Emergency Landing 紧急迫降

C: Ladies and gentlemen, your captain speaking. We are suffering a technical problem,

Unit 5 Emergency Handling 紧急情况处理

for everyone's safety we decide to land in the next 20 minutes at the nearest airport. The landing is perfectly normal, but for safety reasons we will evacuate the aircraft using the slides. The cabin crew will give you necessary instructions and help you prepare for the landing. Please listen to their instructions carefully. Thank you.

M: Ladies and gentlemen. As what the captain has just told you, we shall be landing in 20 minutes. For safety reasons, after landing we shall be leaving the aircraft using the evacuation slides. So please listen carefully and do as exactly as our instructions. Please return to your seats immediately and keep your seat belts fastened securely.

We are going to take you through our safety procedures. Please watch and listen carefully. The safety card in your seat pocket shows the details of escape routes, oxygen masks and life jackets for you. It also shows the bracing position, which you must adopt while an emergency landing. Again, please listen carefully…

Please remain seated and follow the instructions given to you by our crew. Do not leave your seats until our crew instruct you. When the seat belt signs are off, go to your nearest exit. Leave all personal belongings behind. I repeat, leave all personal hand baggage behind. Ladies, remove your high-heeled shoes, as they may tear the slide.

P: Excuse me, what is happening, are we going to crash?

A: Of course not. We'll be on the ground. Don't worry, our crews are well trained to handle the situation, please follow our instructions.

P: OK.

（2）Emergency Exits　应急出口

(PA is in progress...)

M: Emergency exits are on both sides of the aircraft. They are clearly marked and are being pointed out to you now.

(Cabin crews are pointing out to the emergency exits.)

M: Please take a moment now to locate the exit nearest to you, bearing in mind that the nearest usable exit may be behind you. To help you find the way to the exits, additional lighting is provided in the aisles at floor level.

P: Do we have emergency exits on the upper deck?

A: On the main deck there are two exits at the rear of the First Class cabin and two at the front and rear of each other cabin sections. On the upper deck there is an emergency exit on each side, in the middle of the cabin.

P: Thank you!

（3）Cabin Decompression　客舱释压

(Cabin pressure falls, and oxygen masks drop down.)

P: What's happening?

A: We're descending to a lower altitude.

M: Ladies and gentlemen, this is an emergency. This is an emergency. Stay in your

seats with your seat belts fastened. Remain calm and follow these instructions. Pull down the oxygen mask. Put it over your nose and mouth immediately and breathe normally.

A: Grab your mask. Pull it down and place it over your nose and mouth.

M: Remain calm. Stay in your seats and pull down a mask towards you. Place the mask over your mouth and nose like this and breathe normally, adjusting the band to secure it. Do make sure your own mask is fitted properly before helping anyone else.

P: I feel fine. Why do I need oxygen?

A: Because the air pressure in the cabin is too low, please use it while we descend to a lower altitude. Keep your mask on until we tell you to take it off. Once we get down to 10,000 feet, we'll make another announcement.

M: We've leveled off at 10,000 feet. We're going to divert to Dalian. You may take off your oxygen masks now. There is really nothing to worry about, but please feel free to ask the cabin crew if you need any assistance before we get to Dalian. After landing we'll make alternative arrangements for you to reach your destinations.

(4) First-aid on Board 机上急救

P: Hey, come here quickly. There's a man. He's unconscious.

A1: OK, where is he? (To A2) Grab the oxygen and a defibrillator from the medical kit and get A3 to call the FSM to advise him a medical emergency.

A2: OK.

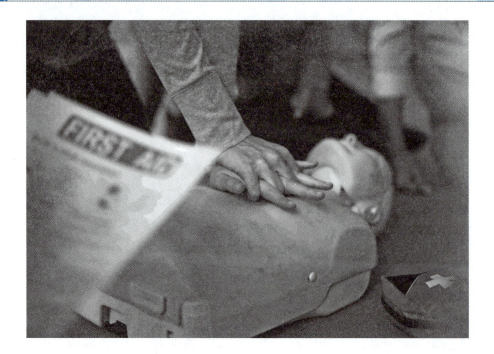

A3: Hello! This is A3 here from Economy cabin. We have a medical emergency on board...

A1: Hello, can you hear me? (to his wife) Are you travelling with this passenger?

W: I'm his wife. Oh my goodness, I think he's had a heart attack. He said he had a bit of indigestion — that was all. He stood up to go to the toilet and then collapsed.

A1: His face is very gray. He's not breathing. Let's put him on the floor now. Oh, he's breathing again. (to the wife) Has this ever happened before?

W: No.

A1: A2, help me put the mask over his head. (to the ill man) Can you hear me?

A1: (to other passengers) Please move away and return to your seats. He needs as much air as possible. (to A2) I think we need a doctor. Can you make an announcement immediately? (to the wife) Is he on any medication?

W: Yes, he's a diabetic so he has injections for that. Is he going to be all right?

A1: Don't worry. We're taking care of him. How old is he?

W: 65.

A1: And is he in good health usually?

W: Yes, but he's been very tired recently.

A2: Ladies and gentlemen, if there is a doctor on board, please make yourself known to the cabin crew immediately by pressing your call bell. Thank you.

D: I'm a doctor, and what's the problem?

W: Oh, thank goodness.

A1: Hello, doctor, thank you for coming. This passenger is unconscious and he stopped breathing a few seconds ago. We administered CPR for two minutes and he's breathing again, although his pulse is very weak and his breathing is shallow. We're just administering oxygen...

5.3 Sentence Patterns
常用句型

Giving instructions 给予指示

Stay in your seats.

Remain calm.

Pull down the oxygen mask.

Put the mask over his head. Tell the captain.

Make an announcement immediately.

Expressing Certainty 表达确定

I bet.../It is bound to.../Of course it will...

I am absolutely sure that you are required to fill in this form.

I am sure it does./I am positive.

I am one hundred percent certain.

I am quite convinced that…

There's no doubt about the arrival.

You must be kidding.

I give you my word for it.

I don't think there is any doubt.

I'm definitely positive.

There is no chance/possibility/hope for sb. to do sth.

There's no room for doubt.

I swear that this is the truth.

Expressing Uncertainty 表达不确定

It all depends.

I can't decide.

I have no idea about...

I suppose it could be...

I was wondering if...

I wouldn't be surprised if...

I cannot say for certain/sure.

It is really difficult to tell that.

I doubt if…/Perhaps…/Maybe...

Expressing Helplessness 表达无能为力

There's nothing I can do about it.

I've no idea how to deal with such a situation.

I don't think I can come up with an idea.

It's beyond my means.

I feel vulnerable about that.

I'm afraid it may be beyond me.

I feel powerless over this.

I'm afraid I can't help with it.

I wish I could find a solution to it.

5.4 Further Reading 扩展阅读

Is there a doctor on board?

Most people who have flown long-distance flights have heard the call: "If there is a medical doctor on board, please identify yourself to a flight attendant." But, believe me, if

Unit 5 Emergency Handling 紧急情况处理

you're a doctor, your first instinct is to hide in the toilet. I know this sort of thing should be second nature to me, but I'm used to working in a hospital with a very small audience. In Economy class, there can be 300 people watching, who are very interested in what's going on. So, when I heard the call, somewhere over the mid-Atlantic, I tried to sink deeper into my seat, hiding my face behind my magazine. But, when nobody else responded, I pushed the call button.

There was a male passenger in the First class with abdominal pain. He was 60 to 70 years old. I performed a brief examination and I concluded that the pain was probably caused by a kidney stone. I gave the man some pain killers and said I'd check on him later.

I tried to sleep, but maybe an hour later the attendant approached me again, "there is another patient for you." Oh dear! It was also an elderly man with a history of heart disease. I asked the attendant if there was a defibrillator on board. The second patient said he had typical chest pain and felt sick at the stomach. Then he was sick and after that he felt a little better. I gave him some medicine for his stomach from the medical kit and then I checked on my first patient and he said he felt a lot better. A couple of hours later, a flight attendant woke me from a deep sleep (this was an overnight flight) to apologetically tell me that there was a third passenger in need of attention. This time it was an elderly lady who was having trouble breathing and the flight attendant had got an oxygen mask on her. Well, her lungs were clear and her pulse was normal and she seemed really panicky, and her travelling companion said she had been under a lot of stress and hated flying. So this was probably a panic attack. I told the flight attendant to keep her on oxygen for another half an hour and told the patient in my most reassuring tone that she would be feeling better soon. I then checked on the kidney stone patient and that sick man. I went back to the galley and had some coffee with the crew, then went back to the panicky lady, who was feeling much better.

The flight crew was very nice and gave me a free bottle of champagne as a gift. But when we landed I decided I would never again admit that I was a doctor on an aircraft flight!

5.5 Group Practice 小组练习

① Cabin crew play an important part in an incident involving US Airways flight 1549 in February 2009. You are going to read a newspaper article about that incident.

- Describe what you can see in the picture?
- What do you know about that incident?
- What factors make it a successful ditching?

② In emergency situations, the crew have to issue direct orders. Listen and underline the main stress on each order. After finishing that work with a partner, please take turns to read the orders loudly and say the main stress.

1. Keep your mask on!
2. Stay calm!
3. Stay in your seat!
4. Keep your seat belt fastened!
5. Don't unfasten your seat belt!
6. Sit down!
7. Breathe normally.
8. Put your own mask on first.
9. Hold on!
10. Don't get up.

Unit 5　Emergency Handling　紧急情况处理

US Airways Flight 1549 lost both engines following a massive bird-strike three and a half minutes after take-off and made an emergency landing in the Hudson River yesterday in the late afternoon. There were 150 passengers and five crew members, including the captain, first officer and three flight attendants, on board. All 155 survived.

The plane ditched at exactly 15.31, less than seven minutes after take-off. Four minutes later all the passengers and crew had been evacuated on to the wings of the floating aircraft or into the slightly submerged slides. They were then taken to safety on Hudson River ferries. Before leaving the aircraft himself, the captain made one last check inside to see that no one was left behind. There were no serious injuries.

Many are calling this a miracle. However, aviation authorities are saying that the real reason for the success of the landing and evacuation was the first-class training of the pilots and cabin crew. They knew what to do and did it superbly.

③ Role Play

A. A passenger seems to have a diarrhea on the airplane and he is running a fever. The stewardess comes to ask if he needs any help.

B. A passenger's baby starts choking on something that seems to have blocked his/her airway. What should the stewardess do?

C. An old passenger has difficulty breathing. None of his family members are with him on the airplane. How should the flight attendants treat him and what arrangements should they make?

5.6 Flight Tips
飞行小贴士

How to protect yourself in the event of cabin depressurization?
中国机长告诉你遇到客舱释压怎样自救

Passengers can take several steps to protect themselves in the event of cabin depressurization. The required steps are simple, but passengers must complete them quickly, especially when the aircraft suddenly loses the cabin pressure.

● Passengers must wear oxygen masks quickly after an airliner loses the cabin pressure, as the effects of hypoxia may impair their ability to do so in a short time. Studies have shown that hypoxia following a sudden loss of the cabin pressure in an airliner at cruise altitude can begin impairing a person's functioning and decision-making in as little as eight seconds. Within 30 seconds, passengers may become so impaired that they are unable to perform simple tasks such as putting on an oxygen mask. Passengers should ensure that the oxygen mask is worn properly so that it

covers both the nose and mouth.

- One way passengers can ensure familiarity with oxygen masks in an emergency is to pay attention to the pre-flight safety briefing and review the safety information card provided by the airline.

- Passengers should also heed the instructions to put on their own oxygen masks before helping others put on their masks. Passengers who have put on their own oxygen masks will be fully capable of helping others in nearby seats, but passengers who do not may become impaired before they are able to help others or themselves.

- In the very rare instance of an explosive decompression, wearing seat belts increases passengers' chances of survival. Seat belts do not provide absolute protection to passengers; media reports indicate that the passenger killed on Southwest Flight 1380 was wearing her seat belt. However, seat belts have protected passengers in some explosive decompression incidents. The most notable such incident involved Aloha Airlines (AQ) Flight 243 in 1988, in which all passengers who had their seat belts fastened survived an explosive decompression that blew off a large portion of the aircraft's forward fuselage.

Unit 6

Cabin Announcements
客舱广播

6.1 Normal Announcements
正常广播

（1）旅客登机时的广播

女士们、先生们：早上好/中午好/下午好/晚上好！

欢迎您乘坐_____航空公司_____次班前往_____。当您登机后，请凭登机牌号码对号入座，座位号码标于两侧行李架的边缘部分。

请将您的手提物品集中于行李架内，或您前排的座位下方。请您不要将行李放在通道或者紧急出口处。请安排好行李的旅客尽快就座，以便让开通道，使后面的旅客尽快进入客舱。

多谢您的合作。

Good morning/afternoon/evening, ladies and gentlemen,

This is _____ heading for _____ via _____. Please take your seat according to the seat number on your boarding pass. Your seat number is indicated on the edge of the overhead compartment. Please make sure your carry-on baggage is in the overhead compartment or under the seat in front of you. Please keep the aisle and the exits clear of baggage. Would you mind stepping aside to clear the aisle for other passengers to pass?

Thank you for your cooperation!

（2）登机门关闭时的广播

女士们、先生们：你们好！

登机门已经关闭。为了保障飞机导航通讯系统正常工作，在飞机起飞和下降过程中请不要使用手提式电脑，在整个航程中请不要使用手提电话、遥控玩具、电子游戏机、激光唱机和电音频接收器等电子设备。

飞机很快就要起飞了，现在由客舱乘务员进行安全检查。请您坐好，系好安全带，收起座椅靠背和小桌板。请您确认您的手提物品是否妥善安放在头顶上的行李架内或座椅下方。本次航班全程禁烟，在飞行途中请不要吸烟。

谢谢。

Ladies and gentlemen,

The door of our aircraft is closed. In order to ensure normal operation of the aircraft navigation and the communication system, passengers are not allowed to use laptop computers toys and other electronic devices throughout the flight and during take-off and landing.

We will take off immediately. Please be seated, fasten your seat belt, and make sure your seat back is straight up, your tray table is folded and your carry-on items are securely stowed in the overhead compartment or under the seat in front of you. This is a non-smoking flight, so please do not smoke on board.

Thank you!

（3）旅客入座后进行客舱设备示范广播（航前安全演示广播）

女士们、先生们：你们好！

现在由客舱乘务员向大家介绍救生衣、氧气面罩、安全带的使用方法和紧急出口的位置。救生衣在您座椅下方/上方。使用时取出，经头部穿好。将带子扣好系紧。然后打开充气阀门，但在客舱内请不要充气。充气不足时，请将救生衣头部的两个人工充气管拉出，用嘴向里充气。请拔出救生衣上的电池插销。

（乘务员进行氧气面罩使用演示）氧气面罩储藏在您座椅的上方。发生紧急情况时面罩会自动脱落。氧气面罩脱落后，请用力向下拉面罩，将面罩罩在口鼻处，把带子套在头上进行正常呼吸。

（乘务员进行安全带使用演示）座位上的安全带在使用时请将连接片插入锁扣内，当飞机起飞、着陆和飞行中遇到颠簸以及"系好安全带"指示灯亮时，请您系好安全带。解开时请您将锁扣打开，然后拉出连接片。

本架飞机除通常出口外，在客舱中部的左、右两侧还有应急出口，分别标有应急出口的明显标志。请记住离您最近的出口。

电源失效，安装在地板上的应急路径灯将发出亮光（指引您至出口），白/蓝色为撤离路径，红色为出口灯。

在您前面座椅背后的口袋里备有安全须知卡，请您仔细阅读。

谢谢！

Ladies and Gentlemen,

Now we will explain the use of the life vest, oxygen mask, seat belt and the location of the exits. Your life vest is in the compartment under your seat/over your head. To put the life vest on, slip it over your head, then fasten the buckles and pull the straps tight around your waist. Then pull the inflation tab. Please do not inflate it while you are in the cabin. If your vest is not inflated enough, you can also inflate it by blowing into the mouth pieces. Pull the battery pin once you leave the plane.

Your oxygen mask is in the compartment over your head. It will drop in front of you automatically when needed. If you see the mask, pull it towards you. Place the mask over your nose and mouth and slip the clastic band over your head. Within a few seconds the oxygen flow will begin.

Please make sure your seat belt is securely fastened during taxing, take-off, landing and encountering air turbulence or when the Fasten Seat Belt signs are ON.

There are emergency exits on both sides of the aircraft in addition to the main entrance doors, and all the exits are clearly marked.

If there is loss of electrical power, the emergency track lights installed near the floor will illuminate. (They lead to Exits.) White/blue lights lead to red lights, which indicate the exits.

For further information, you will find a leaflet of safety instruction in the seat pocket in front of you.

Thank you.

Unit 6　Cabin Announcements　客舱广播

（4）飞机滑行即将起飞的广播

女士们、先生们：早上好/中午好/下午好/晚上好！

欢迎您乘坐_____航空公司航班_____前往_____（中途降落_____）。由_____至_____的飞行距离是_____，预计空中飞行时间为_____小时_____分。飞行高度_____米，飞行速度为平均每小时_____千米。

为了保障飞行导航通讯系统正常工作，在飞机起飞和下降过程中请不要使用手提式电脑，在整个航程中请不要使用手提电话、遥控玩具、电子游戏机、激光唱机和电音频接收机等电子设备。

飞机很快就要起飞了，请您坐好，系好安全带，收起小桌板。请您确认您的手提物品是否妥善地安放在头顶上方的行李架内或座椅下方。本次航班全程禁烟，在飞行途中请不要吸烟。

本次航班乘务长将协同所有乘务员竭诚为您提供及时周到的服务。

谢谢。

Good morning/afternoon/evening, ladies and Gentlemen,

Welcome aboard _____ Airline flight _____ to _____ (via _____). The distance between _____ and _____ is _____ kilometers. Our flight will take _____ hours and _____ minutes. We will be flying at an altitude of _____ meters and the average speed is _____ kilometers per hour.

In order to ensure normal operation of the aircraft navigation and the communication system, passengers are not allowed to use laptop computers, toys and other electronic devices throughout the flight and during take-off and landing.

We will take off immediately. Please be seated, fasten your seat belt, and make sure your seat back is straight up, your tray table is folded and your carry-on items are securely stowed in the overhead compartment or under the seat in front of you. This is a non-smoking flight, so please do not smoke on board.

The (chief) purser with all crew members will be sincerely at your service. We hope you'll enjoy the flight.

Thank you.

（5）飞机进入平飞阶段的客舱以及航行介绍（起飞后5分钟）

女士们、先生们：

我们的飞机已经离开 _____ 前往 _____，沿这条航线，我们飞经的省份有 _____，经过的主要城市有 _____，我们还将飞越 _____。在这段旅途中，我们为您准备了 _____ 餐。供餐时我们将广播通知您。

下面将向您介绍客舱设备的使用方法。今天您乘坐的是 _____ 型飞机。

您的座椅靠背可以调节，调节时请按座椅扶手上的按钮。在您前方座椅靠背上的口袋里有清洁袋，供您扔杂物时使用。

在您座椅的上方备有阅读灯开关和呼唤按钮。如果您需要乘务员的帮助，请按呼唤铃。

在您座椅上方还有空气调节设备，如果您需要新鲜空气，请转动通风口。

洗手间在飞机的前部和后部，在洗手间内请不要吸烟。

谢谢。

Ladies and Gentlemen,

We have left _____ for _____. Along this route, we will be flying over the provinces of _____, passing the cities of _____, and crossing over the _____. Breakfast (lunch, supper) has been prepared for you. We will inform you before we serve it.

Now we are going to introduce you the use of the cabin installations.

This is a _____ aircraft.

The back of your seat can be adjusted by pressing the button on the arm of your seat.

The ventilator is also above your head. By adjusting the airflow knob, fresh air will flow into the ventilations.

Lavatories are located in the front and rear of the cabin. Please do not smoke in the lavatories.

Thank you.

（6）供餐前的广播

女士们、先生们：

我们将为您提供餐食（点心餐）、茶水、咖啡和饮料。欢迎您选用。需要用餐的旅客，请您将小桌板放下。

为了方便其他旅客，在供餐期间，请您将座椅靠背调整到正常位置。

谢谢。

Ladies and Gentlemen,

We will be serving you a meal/snacks with tea, coffee and other soft drinks. Welcome to make your choice. Please unfold the tray table in front of you. For convenience of the passengers behind you, please return your seat to the upright position during the meal service.

Thank you!

（7）飞机降落后的广播

女士们、先生们：

飞机已经降落在 _____ 机场，当地时间为 _____，外面的温度是 _____ 摄氏度或华氏 _____ 度，飞机正在滑行，为了您和他人的安全，请先不要站起来或打开行李架。等飞机停稳、系好安全带的指示灯灭后，再解开安全带，整理好手提物品准备下飞机。从行李架里取物品时，请注意安全。您托运的行李请到行李提取处领取。需要转机的旅客请您到候机楼出发大厅办理登机手续。

继续前往 _____ 的旅客，请您稍后下机，下机时请携带好所有的行李物品。下机后请和地面商务联系接取站登机牌，并留意候机楼广播通知。

感谢您选择 _____ 航空公司班机！下次旅途再会！

Ladies and Gentlemen,

Our plane has landed at _____ Airport. The local time is _____. The temperature outside is _____ degrees Centigrade or _____ degrees Fahrenheit. The plane is taxing. For your safety, please stay in your seat for the time being. When the aircraft stops completely and the Fasten Seat Belt sign is off, please detach the seat belt, take all your carry-on items and disembark. Take care when opening the overhead compartment. Your checked baggage may be claimed in the baggage claim area. Transit passengers please proceed to the departure hall in the terminal building to arrange for your connecting flight.

Passengers continuing the flight with us, please take all your personal belongings with you to obtain your transit boarding pass in the terminal later. Please pay attention to the announcement in the terminal.

Thank you for selecting _____ Airline for your travel today and we look forward to serving you again.

Wish you a pleasant day.

Thank you.

（8）旅客下飞机时的广播

女士们、先生们：早上好/中午好/下午好/晚上好！

欢迎您坐 _____ 航空公司航班，感谢您（鞠躬）在这段旅途中对我们工作的支持和配合，为了帮助我们不断提高服务质量，敬请留下宝贵意见，谢谢您的关心和支持！

Good morning/afternoon/evening, ladies and gentlemen,

Welcome aboard _____ Airline. We would like to thank you for your support and cooperation during this flight. Comments from you will be highly valued in order to improve our service. Thanks for your concern and support!

6.2 Special Announcements
特殊广播

（1）不同情况下航班延误的广播

女士们、先生们：

我们接到机长的通知，由于下述原因（之一/二）：

① 目的地机场/出发地机场天气状况不佳；

② 机械故障，需要维修；

③ 部分旅客尚未登机/旅客乘机手续尚未办妥；

④ 等待中转/转机旅客；

⑤ 货物加重/行李装载/货物装载；

⑥ 临时增加食品/等候食品装载；

⑦ 文件交接工作尚未完成；

⑧ 几位旅客临时取消行程，出于安全考虑，地面工作人员正在查找他们的行李；

⑨ 发动机漏油。

飞机将推迟 _____ 小时 _____ 分后起飞，请您在座位上休息，请不要抽烟。现在乘务员会为您提供饮料/餐食/点心，如有进一步的消息，我们将及时通知您。

谢谢。

Ladies and Gentlemen,

Attention please, we get notice from the captain that:

① Because of bad weather conditions on our scheduled route/over the airport;

② As there is a technical problem that is now being corrected;

③ As we are waiting for (a) passenger(s) who has (have) not joined us on time /As the boarding formalities of (a) passenger(s) are not completed;

④ As we are waiting for interline passengers;

⑤ As we need more time for loading of cargo/baggage;

⑥ We are waiting for catering;

⑦ Due to the late arrival of the important documents;

⑧ As some of the passengers temporarily cancelled their trip, we have to unload their checked baggage;

⑨ Owing to oil leakage of this airplane;

Our flight will be delayed for about _____. Please remain in your seat and do not smoke. Now we will supply beverages/dinner/snacks. We will inform you of further details as soon as possible.

Thank you for your cooperation.

（2）飞机遇到颠簸气流的广播

女士们、先生们：

我们的飞机受气流影响有些颠簸，请您回原位坐好、系好安全带。正在用餐的旅客，请您小心餐桌上的饮料，以免颠簸时洒在衣服、手上。在系好安全带指示灯熄灭

之前，洗手间暂停使用。在这段时间内，我们将停止一切服务供应。

谢谢！

Ladies and Gentlemen,

We have met with some turbulence. Please return to your seat and fasten your seat belt. For the passengers having your meals please take care of your drinks. Please don't use the lavatories until the Fasten Seat Belt sign goes off. Cabin service will be suspended.

（3）有重病人、备降的广播

女士们、先生们：

我们很抱歉地通知大家，现在机上有一重病人，机长决定备降 _____ 机场，我们将在 _____ 小时 _____ 分钟后到达 _____ 。请协助。

Ladies and Gentlemen,

May I have your attention please? There is a serious sick passenger on board, and the captain has decided to make an emergency landing at _____ Airport. We expect to arrive there in _____ hours and _____ minutes. Thank you for cooperation.

（4）遇客舱起火的广播

女士们、先生们：

现在客舱内有一处失火，请大家不要惊慌，我们正在组织灭火。火源附近的旅客请调换一下座位，其他旅客请不要来回走动，请听从乘务员指挥。

谢谢。

Ladies and Gentlemen,

A minor fire has broken out in the cabin, which we are putting out. The passengers sitting near the fire, please change your seats to avoid the fire. Other passengers do not leave your seats, and follow our crew's instructions.

Thank you!

（5）发生客舱失压的广播

女士们、先生们：

现在飞机客舱失压，正在紧急下降，请保持镇定，系好安全带，氧气面罩已自动脱落，请您用力拉下氧气面罩，罩在口鼻处，进行正常呼吸，请不要走动。

谢谢。

Ladies and gentlemen,

Your attention please, our plane is undergoing depressurization. Please keep calm. Your oxygen mask has dropped from the unit above your seat. Please fasten your seat belt, reach up and pull the mask down to your face, cover your nose and mouth and slip the elastic band over your head.

Thank you.

（6）准备紧急迫降的乘务长广播

女士们、先生们：

我是本架飞机的乘务长_____。如同机长所述，我们已决定采取陆上/水上迫降，我们全体乘务员都受过良好的训练，请所有旅客回到座位坐好，保持安静，并听从乘务员的指挥。

谢谢！

Ladies and gentlemen,

This is your chief purser speaking. Our situation is as that the captain has just announced. It is necessary to make an emergency landing/ditching. The crew has been well trained to handle this type of situation. We will do everything necessary to ensure your safety. All passengers please return to your seats, keep calm, and pay attention to the directions of the flight attendants.

Thank you!

（7）防止冲击的姿势介绍广播（乘务员规范动作示范）

女士们、先生们：

现在乘务员将向您介绍几种防冲撞姿势。

当您听到防冲撞指令时，请把两腿分开，两脚用力蹬地，两臂交叉，身体前倾，两手抓住前面的座椅靠背，头靠在双臂之上。

如果您的手无法抓到您前面的座椅靠背或者您的前面没有座椅，请弯下腰，双手抓住您的双脚，把头埋在双膝之中。如果您抓不到脚踝，请改抱住双膝。

当您听到"低下头，全身紧缩用力"的口令时请采取这种姿势，直到听到"解开安全带"的口令。

在飞机着陆/水时，会有多次撞击，请保持您的防冲撞姿势直到飞机完全停稳。

现在我们开始练习。

Ladies and gentlemen,

Now the flight attendants will explain to you the brace position to against impact.

When you hear the brace command, put your legs apart, place your feet flat on the floor. Cross your arms like this. Lean forward, and hold the seat back, rest your face on your arms.

If you can't hold the seat back, or there is not a seat back in front of you, please bend over and grab your ankles. If you cannot grab your ankles, grab your knees.

Take this position when you hear "heads down, brace" until you hear "release your seat belts!"

While landing/ditching, the aircraft will impact for several times. Please take your brace position until the aircraft comes to a complete stop.

Now let's practice.

（8）紧急着陆前的广播

女士们、先生们：

根据机长的指示，请做好安全姿势，在飞机落地后未停稳之前，仍保持原来的姿势。撤离时，请听从乘务员的指挥。

飞机马上就要着陆/水上迫降，请再次确认安全带是否系好及您的安全姿势。

谢谢！

Ladies and gentlemen,

Our captain instructs all passengers to brace now for landing/ditching and to remain in this position until the aircraft comes to a full stop. For evacuation, please follow the instructions of the crew.

We will be landing/ditching immediately, please make sure your seat belt is fastened securely and brace correctly.

Thank you!

（9）延误的广播

女士们、先生们：

本架飞机已经降落在_____机场，外面温度为_____摄氏度或_____华氏度。由机场到市区距离_____千米。由于_____的原因，延误了您的旅行，我们再次向您表示歉意。飞机还将继续滑行，等"系好安全带"指示灯熄灭后，请您再解开安全带,整理好全部手提物品准备下飞机。您交托运的行李请到出口处领取,中国民航配有班车送您进市区。需在本港转乘飞机的旅客,请您在候机楼办理转乘手续。

在这段旅途中,对于您给予的大力支持与配合我们表示衷心的感谢,并欢迎您再次选择乘坐_____航空公司的航班。

各位旅客,下次旅途再会!

谢谢!

Ladies and gentlemen,

We have just landed at _____ Airport. The temperature outside is _____ degrees Centigrade or _____ degrees Fahrenheit. The distance between the airport and downtown is _____ kilometers. We apologize for the delay in the flight. Please do not unfasten your seat belts before the Fasten Seat Belt sign goes off. Please make sure to collect all your belongings before you disembark. Your checked baggage may be claimed in the

terminal building. CAAC has a coach service operating between the airport and its downtown office. If you wish to take advantage of it, please contact with our ground attendants.

We thank you for flying with _____ Airlines and hope to have the pleasure of being with you again.

Thank you and good-bye!

Unit 7

Knowledge Extension
知识拓展

7.1 Typical Aircraft
飞机机型

Airbus A300 Short to Medium-Range Jetliner

During the mid-1960s, a number of European governments and aircraft manufacturers discussed the possibility of pooling resources to develop a short-range commercial jetliner. After studying a number of potential designs, their attention focused on the HBN-100 being developed by Hawker Siddeley in Britain as well as Bregeut and Nord in France. Finally, France and West Germany agreed to proceed with the project forming what would become known as European Airbus Industrie. Eventually, the conglomerate would come to consist of Hawker Siddeley (now part of British Aerospace), Aerospatiale in France, DASA in Germany, and CASA in Spain with Fokker in the Netherlands and Belairbus in Belgium as major subcontractors. The first design they agreed to construct was a twin-engined wide-body airliner to fill a niche between the Boeing 707 and Boeing 727 seating between 220

and 330 passengers. This design would become known as the A300. Although of the typical airliner layout with a cylindrical fuselage and mid-set swept-wing, the A300 incorporated a number of advanced features for its time, including a wing full of high-lift devices and quiet, fuel-efficient engines. Despite slow initial sales, the A300 gradually made inroads into the airline industry and was being operated throughout Europe, the Middle East, Asia, and North America within a decade. Production of the upgraded A300-600 series continues with over 300 built by 2001.

Airbus A340 Long-Range Jetliner

Designed as a four-engined long-range complement to the A330, the A340 competes primarily with Boeing 777 and 747. The A340 shares many features with the A330, including the same fuselage, landing gear, tail assembly, flight deck, and basic wing. The wing structure and leading-edge slats are slightly modified because of the two additional engines. The two major versions of the A340 in service are the basic A340-300 and the extended-range A340-200. In addition, a combined passenger/freight A340-300 model has also been developed. Current efforts are focused on the new A340-600 with a longer fuselage for up to 410 (and possibly 550) passengers and much more powerful engines. A shorter A340-500 with enlarged wings and increased fuel capacity is planned to complement the A340-600 and offer even greater range. Nearly 200 examples of the A340 had been built by 2001.

Airbus A380（A3XX）Long-Range Jetliner

With airports becoming ever more congested and air traffic control systems struggling to keep up with the increasing number of aircraft in operation, Airbus began development of its solution, the A3XX. Once officially launched in late 2000, Airbus rechristened the design the A380. If the proposed airliner does indeed enter service, it will become the first full triple-decked super jumbo-jet as well the first challenge to Boeing's monopoly on very large aircraft. Though many argue that the industry is not ready for such a design, Airbus believes that by committing to the A380 now, they will be in excellent position to take advantage of such a need by 2020. Despite its large size, the A380 is of typical airliner layout with a cylindrical fuselage slightly shorter and wider than the rival Boeing 747 and four podded engines along the wing. Because of customer-imposed constraints, the A380 will also be able to use existing runways and gates, and folding wings may also be offered to some airlines. Internal layout is also of typical configuration with passengers seated on the two upper decks and cargo on the lower deck. Airbus has also proposed using some cargo compartments for shops and lounges, although economy-minded airlines are unlikely to adopt such gimmicks. Two basic models are currently being marketed, the A380-800 (formerly A3XX-100) passenger model seating up to 555 in three classes and the A380-800F (formerly A3XX-100F) freighter version. Additional extended range, passenger/cargo, and stretched models

are also under consideration. If all goes according to plan, the first A380 will enter service sometime in 2005 or 2006.

Boeing B737 Short to Medium-Range Jetliner

The Boeing 737 concept was first rooted in 1964 and was to be a low-cost solution derived from the Boeing 727 and Boeing 707, with the first aircraft being produced in 1967. The original 737-100 was short and stocky, but over the following forty-odd years, eight more variants have been produced. Seating capacity has grown from 85 to 215 passengers.

The production has been so prolific that as of July 2015, 8,599 aircraft have been produced with the order book standing at 4,253 aircraft still to be delivered. On average there are 1,250 Boeing 737s airborne at any given time with 2 landing or departing every 5 seconds.

The nine variants of the Boeing 737 are split into two generations of aircraft. The Classic Series consists of the Boeing 737-100, Boeing 737-200, Boeing 737-300, Boeing 737-400 and Boeing 737-500 variants, while the Next Generation Series includes the Boeing 737-600, Boeing 737-700, Boeing 737-800 and Boeing 737-900ER variants. The Next Generation saw improvements to the wing design, upgraded cockpit as well as a modernization of the interior. Being the only narrow-body aircraft now being produced by Boeing, the 737 has replaced the Boeing 707, 727, 757 as well as the DC9, MD80 and MD90. The main competition for the Boeing 737 today is the Airbus A320 family of aircraft. One of the 737s' advantages over these rivals was its wider cabin allowing for a 6 abreast seating layout as compared to 5 abreast offered by its rivals.

The Boeing 737-100 and Boeing 737-200 variants were powered by Pratt and Whitney JT8D-1 engines which were wing-mounted. These engines were low bypass engines and were distinctive in the way they sat under the wing-like a pipe extending forward and aft of the wing. The reverse thrust was provided by half-shells that extended back over the exhaust tailpipe and redirected air forward over and under the wing. The Boeing 737-300 was the first major rethink of the aircraft design with a longer fuselage, greater wingspan and new engines. The CFM56-3B-1 high-bypass turbofan was chosen, and to solve the problem of low ground clearance the engine was placed forward of the wing on a pylon attached to the wing. In addition, engine accessories were placed on the sides rather under the engine which made the nacelles slightly triangular rather than circular when viewed from the front.

The Next Generation family of variants delivered various improvements in technology:

more efficient engines, improved aerodynamics, increased passenger capacity, longer range and electronic cockpits.

Boeing B747 Long-range Jetliner

The Boeing 747 is a wide-body commercial airliner and its nickname is "Jumbo Jet". It is among the world's most recognizable aircraft and was the first wide body ever produced. Manufactured by Boeing's Commercial Airplane in the US, the original version of the 747 was two and a half times the size of the Boeing 707, one of the common large commercial aircraft of the 1960s. First flown commercially in 1970, the 747 held the passenger capacity record for 37 years.

The four-engine 747 uses a double deck configuration for part of its length. It is available in passenger, freighter and other versions. Boeing designed the 747's hump-like upper deck to serve as a first class lounge or (as is the general rule today) extra seating, and to allow the aircraft to be easily converted to a cargo carrier by removing seats and installing a front cargo door. Boeing did so because the company expected supersonic airliners whose development was announced in the early 1960s to render the 747 and other subsonic airliners obsolete, but that the demand for subsonic cargo aircraft would be robust into the future. The 747 in particular was expected to be sold well but it exceeded its critics' expectations with production passing the 1,000 mark in 1993. As of October 2008, 1,409 aircrafts had been built and 115 more in various configurations on order.

Boeing B777 Long-Range Jetliner

The Boeing 777 was designed in consultation with eight leading airlines and was designed to replace the ageing McDonnell Douglas DC-10 and Lockheed L1011 Tristar. It also provided a capacity bridge between the Boeing 767 and the Boeing 747. The original 777 offering was the Boeing 777-200 version which was followed up in 1997 by the Boeing 777-200ER where the ER stands for Extended Range. In 1998 Boeing introduced the stretched Boeing 777-300 variant which was 10.1 meters (33.3 feet) longer than the Boeing 777-200 series. The long-range variant, the Boeing 777 300ER was added in 2004 with the longer-range Boeing 777-200LR rolling off the line in 2006. Boeing has also introduced a freighter version which was first delivered in 2009. The Boeing 777 is Boeing's best-selling aircraft. In a market currently focused heavily on fuel savings, a large fuel-efficient twin jet is a very attractive offering. The main competition for the Triple Seven is Airbus A330, Airbus A340 and the Airbus A350.

As Boeing deliver its 1,000th 777, they are working hard to ensure the longevity and relevance of this very popular air-frame. The next generation of 777s is on the drawing board and currently is known as the 777X.

The 777X is expected to have a wingspan exceeding today's 777-300ER by 6 meters (6 feet). The folding wingtips are designed to enable the 777X to use airport gates designed for current 777 variants. They would be locked in place for takeoff and flight. The extended wings allow better fuel economy and speed.

7.2 Famous Airlines
著名航空公司

American Airlines 美利坚航空公司

American Airlines is the largest airline in the world and is based in Fort Worth, Texas in the United States. Its IATA designator is AA. In 1934, American Airways Company became American Airlines, Inc. It is now one of the divisions operated by its parent company, AMR

Corp.

AMR Corp. also operates American Eagle Airlines, Inc. (which includes Executive Air) and American Connection. Trans World Airlines, LLC was operated by AMR before it was consolidated into AA. American Airlines is part of the Airline Alliance Oneworld. They also code share rail service to stations in France with SNCF French Rail, Belgium with Thalys International, Germany with Deutsche Bahn (Airail Service) and stations in Switzerland (one of which also serves France), with Swiss Rail.

American Airlines developed from a conglomeration of about 82 small airlines companies through a series of corporate acquisitions and reorganizations. In 1934, American Airways Company, in financial straits, was acquired by a corporate raider, E L. (Errett Lobban) Cord, who renamed the company "American Airlines". Early in its history, it was headquartered at Midway Airport in Chicago, Illinois. The main American Airlines route until the late 1950s was from New York and Chicago to Los Angeles via Dallas. One of the early American Airlines presidents, C. R. (Cyrus Rowlett) Smith worked closely with Donald Douglas to develop the DC-2, which American Airlines started flying in 1936. After World War II, American launched an international subsidiary, American Overseas Airways, to serve Europe. It also launched flights to Mexico in the 1940s. With the introduction of jet service in the 1960s, Americans focus shifted to nonstop coast-to-coast flights, although it maintained feeder connections to other cities along its old route. During the 1970s, American flew to Australia and New Zealand although it traded these routes to Pan Am in 1975 in exchange for routes to the Caribbean. In the 1980s, American began flights to Europe and Japan. American Airlines moved its corporate headquarters from New York City to Fort Worth, Texas in 1979, and changed its routing to a spoke-hub distribution paradigm starting in 1981. Its official hubs since then have been:

- Dallas/Fort Worth International Airport (1981-present)
- Chicago/O' Hare International Airport (1982-present)
- Nashville International Airport (1986-1995)
- Raleigh-Durham International Airport (1987-1996)
- San Jose International Airport (1988-1995)
- San Juan Luis Munoz Marin International Airport (1987-present)
- Miami International Airport (1990-present)

San Juan was added to the network in the Pan Am trade. Miami was added when American purchased the Latin American operations of Eastern Airlines in 1991, making it the largest U. S. carrier in that region.

United Airlines 美国联合航空公司

United Airlines (UAL) is an American airline, the second largest in the world. Based in Elk Grove, Illinois, near Chicago, it employs around 84,000 people and operates around 540 aircraft (Jan 2002). In 1994, 55% of company stock was given to employees as part of a pay cut, called ESOP (Employee Stock Ownership Plan). This made it the largest employee-owned company in the world. The shares have now been sold for pennies on the dollar, and the ESOP program has been terminated. In 2001 the company lost $2,137 million on revenues of $16,138 million and in 2002 the company was forced into bankruptcy protection. It is set to emerge in the first half of 2004.

United Airlines has the United Express airline contracted to perform its regional flying. UA is part of the Star Alliance and currently code shares with SNCF French Rail to stations in France. Its TATA designator is UA.

UAL originated in the air mail service of Walter Varney, founded in 1926. In only four years the company included a number of airlines, aero manufacturing companies and several airports and was also closely associated with the new firm of William Boeing. Following the Air Mail Scandal of 1930, by 1934 the company still held its airline routes but had lost all its non-airline holdings. United's early routes centered around the West Coast, Midwest, and Mid-Atlantic states. It operated transcontinental flights through Denver, Colorado, which remains a major united hub to this day. During World War II United was involved in the training of ground crews and material transportation. Post-war United benefited from the boom in demand for air travel. The company merged with Capital Airlines on June 1, 1961, making it the world's largest commercial airline and giving it a route network covering the entire United States. In 1968 the company reorganized, creating UAL, Inc., with United as a wholly owned subsidiary. United also began to seek overseas routes in the 1960s, but the

Transpacific Route Case (1969) denied them this expansion and it did not gain an overseas route until 1983, when they began flights to Tokyo. By the end of the year, United had flights to 13 Pacific destinations, many of which were with route contracts purchased from the ailing Pan Am. The economic turmoil from the 1970s and the pressures of the Airline Deregulation Act (1978) affected the company, with losses and a greatly increased turnover in top management. The company also diversified and changed its name twice before returning to its airline business in 1987. In 1990 the company initially expanded aggressively, purchasing Pan Am's rights at London Heathrow Airport and paving the way for the company's first trans-Atlantic flights. However, the aftermath of the Gulf War and increased competition led to losses of $332 m in 1991 and $957 m in 1992.

In 1997 it joined the Star Alliance with Air Canada, Lufthansa, SAS and Thai Airways. It was among the first to introduce the Boeing 777 twin-jet on trans Atlantic routes. In December of 2002, UAL Corporation filed for Chapter 11 protection against bankruptcy. On November 12, 2003, United Airlines launched a new low-cost carrier, Ted.

United has hub operations at O'Hare International Airport in Chicago, Illinois; Denver International Airport near Denver, Colorado, Dulles International Airport in Chantilly, Virginia and Dulles, Virginia, San Francisco International Airport in San Francisco, California and Los Angeles International Airport in Los Angeles, California. United also has significant operations at Miami International Airport in Miami, Florida, London Heathrow Airport in London, UK and New Tokyo International Airport in Narita, Japan.

British Airways 英国航空公司

British Airways or BA is the largest airline of the United Kingdom and one of the largest in the world. Its IATA designator is BA. It was formed in 1974 from the merger of the state owned British Overseas Airways Corporation and British European Airways (BEA). During the fiscal year ending 2002, BA carried 40 million passengers on revenues exceeding GBP 8 billion. The flag carrier was privatized and floated on the London Stock Exchange in 1987 by the Conservative government of Mrs. Thatcher. The airline has British Airways City express, Duo Airways, and Logan air as its subsidiaries.

British Airways is based at the London Heathrow Airport. It also has a commanding presence at Gatwick. BA has succeeded in dominating Heathrow to the point that the airport is commonly referred to as Fortress Heathrow within both the airline and its competitors. As an incumbent airline, BA had grandfather rights to around 36% of takeoff and landing

slots at Heathrow, many of which are used for the lucrative trans-Atlantic market. Some competitors, such as Virgin Atlantic, British Midland and United Airlines, assert that this stifles competition and some political think tanks recommend an auction of slots. In recent years British Airways has been buying slots from other airlines including United Airlines, DAT, Virgin Atlantic, and Swissair, and now owns about 40% of slots at Heathrow.

British Airways was an operator of the famous Aerospatiale-BAC Concorde supersonic airliner. BA had a daily Concorde service between London and New York. On October 24, 2003, they ceased scheduled services with Concorde, due to depressed passenger numbers and increasing maintenance costs. The last day of its Saturday-only London Heathrow to Barbados Concorde flight was on August 30, 2003. British Airways aircraft use the Airline call sign "Speed Bird" in ATC radio transmissions. The airline's IATA designator is BA. British Airways is a founding member of the Oneworld Airline Alliance.

Air France   法国航空公司

Air France (AFR, Company National Air France) is the national airline of France with the IATA designation: AF. The company transported 43.3 million passengers and earned 12.53 billion Euro in revenues between April 2001 and March 2002. It has routes to 296 cities in 85 countries and employs over 64,000 people. It is part of the Skyteam Alliance with Delta, Aeromexico, Korean Air, Czech Airlines and Alitalia. The company fleet consists of around 240 aircraft, 100 from Boeing (mainly long haul) and 14 from Airbus. Five Concords were withdrawn from use early in 2003.

Founded on August 30, 1933 through the merger of Air Orient, Company General Aeropostale, Society General de Transport Aerien (SGTA, the first French carrier, founded as Lignes Aeriennes Farman in 1919), Air Union and CIDNA (Company International de Navigation). The airline had extensive routes across Europe, but also to French colonies

in northern Africa and elsewhere. The company was nationalized in 1946, and Company National Air France was created by a parliamentary act on June 16, 1948. The government held 70% of the new company and still (mid-2002) holds a 54% stake in the airline. On August 4, 1948, Max Hymans was appointed president of Air France. During his thirteen years at the helm, he implemented a modernization policy based on jet aircraft, specifically the "Caravelle" and the Boeing 707. In 1949 the company was one of the founders of SITA (Society International de Telecommunications Aeronautiques). The airline used the De Havilland Comet for a short while from 1953, but soon replaced them with Viscounts and in 1959 the company started widespread use of the elegant twin-jet Sud Aviation Caravelle. It graduated to the use of Boeing aircraft, but as a national European carrier it became committed to Airbus designs from 1974. First available in 1976, the airline operated the unique Concorde SST supersonic airliner, using it on the Paris-Charles de Gaulle to New York route as well as a number of other routes (those other routes were dropped in 1982).

On September 30, 2003, Air France and Netherlands-based KLM Royal Dutch Airlines, announced the merging of the two airlines, forming a new company to be known as Air France-KLM. Air France shareholders will own 81 per cent of the new firm while KLM shareholders will hold the rest. The French government's share of Air France will be reduced from 54.4 per cent to 44 per cent.

Lufthansa 德国汉莎航空公司

Lufthansa is the name of German National Airline Company, headquartered in Cologne. Their main base is Frankfurt. Lufthansa is a founding member of Star Alliance, one of the world's major airline alliances. Currently, the Lufthansa Group operates more than 300 aircraft. It uses the IATA designator LH.

The company was founded in 1926, following a merger between "Deutsche Aero Lloyd"

Lufthansa

(DAL) and "Junkers Luftverkehr" on January 6 of that year. Its original name was Deutsche Lufthansa Aktiengesellschaft.

In 1997 Lufthansa was a founding member of the Star Alliance. At the end of 2001 the Lufthansa Group's fleet comprised 334 jets with an average age of 8.1 years. Lufthansa is one of the world's largest international carriers with more than 29 million of its 44 million passengers in 2001 crossing national boundaries. Services from London Heathrow, Manchester, Edinburgh, Birmingham, Newcastle, Dublin and London City connect conveniently and competitively into their extensive world-wide network serving more than 100 destinations in Europe and 330 destinations worldwide. In a collaborative development program with Boeing, a Lufthansa 747-400 has become the world's first airliner with broadband internet connectivity onboard. Trials will begin early in 2003 to assess customer preferences in preparation for the airline's entire long haul fleet to be equipped.

Lufthansa's two hubs at Frankfurt and Munich offer efficient and hassle-free connections with all Lufthansa flights arriving and leaving from the same Terminal. The development of Lufthansa's two-hub strategy to expand its long-haul connections from Frankfurt and Munich is backed by a major investment in a second terminal at Munich. Scheduled to open in summer 2003, it has been designed and built in partnership between Lufthansa and Munich Airport for the exclusive use of Lufthansa and its Star Alliance partners.

Lufthansa pioneered Quick Check-in machines to beat the queues when travelling with hand luggage only exit—the new technology for paperless travel-makers travelling more convenient as well. It can't be lost or left behind and it is extremely flexible, so changes can be made at short notice before departure. Exit fares are discounted and currently available in the UK from London Heathrow, London City, Manchester and Birmingham.

Japan Airlines 日本航空公司

Japan Airlines (or JAL) is the national airline company of Japan, along with All Nippon Airways. Its ATA designator is JL. Most of the airline's international service is based at New Tokyo International Airport in Narita, Japan. The domestic service is mostly out of Tokyo International Airport in the ward of Ota in Tokyo, Japan.

Japan Airlines was established in 1951, with the government of Japan recognizing the need for a reliable air transportation system to help Japan grow in the aftermath of World War II. Towards the end of 1950s, it started its first international service, to San Francisco. In 1960, Japan Airlines bought their first jet, a DC-8. Soon after, they decided to re-equip their airline, using jet airplanes only. That decade, many new international destinations were established. In the 1970s they bought the Boeing 747, the Boeing 727 and the McDonnell Douglas DC-10 to accommodate the ever growing list of international routes, both to its Asian neighbors, and around the world. During that decade they also began to be more promotionally aware, with plane models and other promotional items being produced in quantity. It also bought new Boeing 767 jets and retired the DC-8's and 727's.

In 1992, Japan Air Charters was established, and in 1997, an agreement with the Walt Disney Company was announced, making Japan Airlines the official airline of Disney Tokyo. That year also, JAL Express had been established, with Boeing 737 aircraft. Japan Airlines acquired Boeing 777's during that decade, and it was named the official airline of the Sydney Olympic Games.

Currently, Japan Airlines is the only Asian airline that flies to Benito Juarez International Airport in Mexico City. The airline flies a long list of other destinations, both domestic and international.

Singapore Airlines 新加坡航空公司

Singapore Airlines is the national airline of Singapore. It uses the IATA call code SQ. Silkair is its subsidiary. Singapore Airlines began as "Malayan Airways" in 1947, flying an Airspeed Consul twin engined airplane between Singapore and Kuala Lumpur, Ipoh, and Penang (two cities and an island of what is now called West Malaysia).

The remainder of the 1940s was a growth period for Malayan Airlines, as was the 1950s. By 1955, Malayan Airlines fleet had grown to include a large number of Douglas DC-3S. In 1963, the creation of the Federation of Malaysia brought a change of name to "Malaysian Airways". In 1966, the name was changed again, this time to "Malaysia Singapore Airlines" (MSA), following Singapore's departure from the Federation of Malaysia the previous year. MSA ceased operations in 1972, when political disagreements between Singapore and Malaysia resulted in the formation of two new airlines; Singapore Airlines and Malaysia Airlines. Singapore's airline company had 10 aircraft at that time. However, Singapore Airlines' hostesses continued to wear the sarong kebaya dress which had previously been used by MSA. While airlines in Western countries shied away from recruiting young women, Singapore Airlines promoted the image of the "Singapore Girl" in its advertising. Singapore Airlines saw rapid growth. During the 1970s, adding many cities in the Indian subcontinent and Asia to the 22 city network it already served, and acquiring Boeing 747 airplanes. During the 1980s, the United States, Canada, and many European cities joined Singapore Airlines route map. During this time, Madrid became the first and only his panic city to be served by Singapore Airlines. In the 1990s, Singapore Airlines began flights to Johannesburg in South Africa, the first African destination for the airline, with the cities of Cape Town and Durban being added. Their Boeing 747s became known as the Megatops, and they ordered Boeing 767 and Airbus equipment to compliment the Megatops.

Singapore Airlines has an enviable reputation in the air transport industry. It is generally regarded as Asia's leading airline and has won "World's Best Airline" and "Airline of the

Year" awards several times. It previously owned 25% of Air New Zealand (diluted to 4.5% after the New Zealand Government bought into the airline to rescue it from bankruptcy) and is a prominent member of the worldwide Star Alliance. Singapore Airlines operates the youngest fleet in Asia, including the Boeing 747-400, and 777. Airbus A-310 and A-340, and is a launch customer for the largest passenger aircraft yet proposed, the Airbus A380.

Qantas 澳大利亚快达航空公司

Qantas is Australia's oldest and biggest airline. It's also the world's second oldest airline. Its IATA designator is QF.

The company was founded on 16 November, 1920 as "Queensland and Northern Territory Aerial Services Limited", but soon became known simply as Qantas, and adopted that name officially. Qantas was nationalized in 1947 by the Australian Labor Party Federal Government. It remained in public ownership for over four decades until the 1990s, and was successfully privatized, with British Airways now owning a significant stake. Since the merger with Australian Airlines in 1995, it has flown an extensive schedule between all Australian capital cities, as well as many regional cities and towns. It also flies many international routes to and from Australia. Qantas has a reputation for being an aggressive competitor in the Australian aviation market over the years, several domestic Australian airlines have gone out of business amid complaints of anti-competitive pricing by Qantas and exorbitant prices on the newly non-competitive routes.

After September 2001, and the collapse of Ansett Airlines, Qantas held a near monopoly on the Australian domestic air travel market. Virgin Blue, a cut-price competitor, has eaten into this market share somewhat, and Qantas has responded by creating a new, cut price subsidiary airline named Jetstar. Qantas hopes that this move will "crowd out" the cut price segment of the market, allowing Qantas to remain the super dominant player in the Australian

domestic aviation market and one of the few profitable full-service airlines in the world. Qantas has attempted to expand into the New Zealand domestic air travel market, first with a shareholding in Air New Zealand, then by a franchise takeover of Ansett New Zealand. As of July 2003, they currently await regulatory approval to purchase a larger (but still minority) stake in Air New Zealand.

Air Canada 加拿大航空公司

Air Canada is Canada's flag air carrier and recognized as one of the world's safest airlines. Air Canada has the IATA designation AC.

Air Canada has several regional partners, including Air Canada Jazz, Air Labrador, Air Georgian, and Central Mountain Air.

There is also a low-cost airline supported by AC called Air Canada Tango. Trans-Canada Airlines (TCA), Air Canada's predecessor, launched its first flight, a Lockheed 10A, on September 1, 1937. It carried two passengers and mail from Vancouver to Seattle. In 1964 the company changed its name to Air Canada and in 1989 became fully privatized. Air Canada provides scheduled and charter air transportation for passengers and cargo to over 150 destinations, vacation packages to over 90 destinations, as well as maintenance, ground handling and training services to other airlines.

In 2000 after acquiring Canada's second largest air carrier, Canadian Airlines, it became the world's twelfth largest commercial airline. As of 2002, Air Canada provides scheduled and chartered passenger jet service directly to 20 Canadian cities, 35 destinations in the United States and 47 cities in Asia, Australia, the Caribbean, Europe, Mexico, the Middle East, India and South America. Air Canada averages nearly 740 flights each day, and serves 23 million customers annually. It is a member in the Star Alliance network.

As of 2002, Air Canada has about 40, 000 employees and 57 aircraft. In 2002 Air Canada had 77 wide-body jets of several types including the Boeing 747 and 767, Airbus A330-300 and A340-300, and 148 narrow-body jets: Airbus A320, A319, A321, Boeing 737 and Canadair Regional Jet.

On 1 April, 2003, Air Canada asked for bankruptcy protection.

Korean Air 大韩航空公司

Korean Air began in 1962 as Korean Air Lines and at that time was owned by the South Korean Government. It replaced the former Korean carrier Korean National Airlines. In 1969 KAL was acquired by the Hanjin Transport Group and became privately owned.

International flights to Hong Kong and China were flown with Boeing 707s until the airline was privatized. In 1973, KAL introduced Boeing 747s on their Pacific routes and started a European service to Paris using the 707s. A new blue-top livery was introduced in 1984 along with its current name: Korean Air. In 1986 Korean Air became the first airline to use the new MD-11 to supplement its new fleet of Boeing 747-400s, As Korean Air grew, it assigned its fleet of MD-11 jets to freighter-only use in addition to 747 freighters.

Its safety record rates a "B", the second highest grade possible, according to Air Rankings Online. Its IATA designator is KE.

Thai Airways International 泰国国际航空公司

THAI began its life as a domestic airline called Thai Airways Company (TAC). TAC was formed in 1951 when the Thai government purchased shares in three small private airlines and amalgamated their fleets in order to create a national airline. Rapid growth followed with air service reaching into formerly-remote provinces of Thailand. Thai Airways

International formed an alliance with Scandinavian Airlines System in 1960, and Thai Airways International was born. TAC remained a separate company and continued to provide service to cities within Thailand.

For the first six years, THAI served 10 regional destinations with propeller-driven aircraft but in 1966 offered the region's first all-jet service. By 1970, THAI were carrying a half million passengers each year and were ranked as Asia's third largest airline.

As the national airline of Thailand operates out of Don Muang Airport in Bangkok and is a member of the Star Alliance network. THAI does not have much of a presence in the United States, as most tourists to the country come from Europe. Lufthansa markets Thai Air-ways in North America.

Emirates 阿联酋航空公司

Emirates is one of the airlines that fly from the United Arab Emirates. It was established in 1985. Its IATA designator is EK. It hubs Dubai International Airport in Dubai, United Arab Emirates.

Emirates flies to 58 different destinations in Europe, Africa, Asia, and Australia. The airline plans to introduce service to North America on 1 July 2004. The airline is considering

South America.

Emirates code shares rail service to stations in France with SNCF French Rail, Emirates code shares rail to Germany on Deutsche Bahn's AiRail service.

Air China　中国国际航空公司

Air China (中国国际航空公司 literally "Chinese International Aviation Company" abbreviated 国航) is the People's Republic of China's state owned and largest commercial airline. It was set up in 1988 upon the sub-division of the Civil Aviation Administration of China (CAAC) to fly international routes although it also operated a few domestic sectors. Its main hub is Beijing Capital International Airport. Further deregulation of the aviation business took place in 1994, enabling foreign investment in airports and facilitating the import of aircraft built outside mainland China. By 1996 our country had 108 airports with scheduled airline services and around 30 different airlines.

Air China's fleet is predominantly sourced from Boeing although some airliners have been acquired from Airbus, including examples of the long range A340. Seven of the airlines Boeing 747 fleet are cargo-carrying aircraft. A couple of Lockheed Hercules aircraft superseded Antonov12s in the freighter role. Four British Aerospace146 "Whisperer" passenger aircraft were returned to the United Kingdom during 2003 and are parked at Southend Airport in Essex. Since the reunification of Hong Kong with the mainland, competition from Cathay Pacific Airways and Dragon Air Cargo on international routes has been allowed to continue.

Aeroflot　俄罗斯航空公司

Aeroflot has been flying for half a century. It has the IATA designator SU.

Aeroflot has a very complex history, and most of it has been shaped by world changes outside the airline's company structure. Aeroflot had to stop flying into the United States once the Cold War began, and many of its records were kept secret by the old Soviet Union.

Aeroflot foresaw the need to buy new and more modern equipment, and upon the break up of the Soviet Union in 1991, it immediately started buying Western equipment, starting with Air bus aircraft.

In 1992, Aeroflot became an open joint stock company, and in 1994, it entered the United States market, with flights to New York's JFK International Airport and San Francisco, California. Aeroflot also became a Boeing customer, adding new, just out of the plant Boeing 767 jet planes. After this makeover, the rate of Aeroflot's safe flights is currently 99.94 per cent.

Unlike many Russian companies, Aeroflot has embraced a new era of superior advantages and technology, it has been able to avoid the post-communism poverty that the country has had to deal with, and has become a safe and reliable international airline whose safety standards match the highest requirements.

Its passenger operations are out of Sheremetyevo International Airport and its cargo operations are out of Domodedovo International Airport. Both airports are located near Moscow, Russia.

Appendix 1　附录1

Galley Facilities

Articles	Chinese Names
Full Meal Cart	整餐车
Full Beverage Cart	整饮料车
Full Appliance Cart	整用具车
Full Supply Cart	整供应品车
Full Alcohol Cart	整酒车
Half Beverage Cart	半饮料车
Half Appliance Cart	半用具车
Half Supply Cart	半供应品车
Half Alcohol Cart	半酒车
Steel Oven Rack	钢烤炉架
Aluminums Food Box	铝餐箱
Plastic Drawer	塑料抽屉
Aluminums Drawer	铝抽屉
Plastic Champagne Tray	塑料香槟酒托盘
Plastic Cup Tray	塑料大杯托
Plastic Cup Tray with Partition	塑料杯隔
China Plate	瓷分餐盘
China Cold Meat or Fish Plate	瓷冷荤/鱼盘
China Bread Plate	瓷面包盘
China Casserole	瓷热食烤盘
China Bowl	瓷沙拉碗
China Butter Dish	瓷黄油盘
China Tea Pot	瓷茶壶
China Coffee Pot	瓷咖啡壶
China Tea/Coffee Saucer	瓷茶杯/咖啡杯杯碟
China Soup Bowl Saucer	瓷汤碗碟
China Soup Bowl with Cover	瓷汤碗加盖

续表

Articles	Chinese Names
China Large Soup Bowl	瓷大汤碗
Porcelain Small Spoon	瓷小调羹
Porcelain Soup Scoop	瓷汤勺
Porcelain Seasoning Handless Cup	瓷汁盅
Porcelain Milk Handless Cup	瓷奶盅
Wine Glass	玻璃葡萄酒杯
Champagne Flute	玻璃香槟酒杯
Brandy Goblet	玻璃白兰地酒杯
Beverage Cup	玻璃饮料杯
Glass Salad Bowl	玻璃沙拉碗
Steel Knife	不锈钢刀
Steel Fork	不锈钢叉
Steel Scoop	不锈钢勺
Steel Coffee Scoop	不锈钢咖啡勺
Big Paper Meal Box	大纸餐盒
Small Paper Meal Box	小纸餐盒
Big Preventable Skid Paper	大防滑纸
Small Preventable Skid Paper	小防滑纸

Appendix 2　附录2

Airlines Codes

中文名称	英文名称	2位代码	3位代码
中国国际航空公司	Air China	CA	CCA
中国北方航空公司	China Northern Airlines	CJ	CBF
中国南方航空公司	China Southern Airlines	CZ	CSN
中国西南航空公司	China Southwest Airlines	SZ	CXN
中国西北航空公司	China Northwest Airlines	WH	CWN
东方航空公司	China Eastern Airlines	MU	CES
厦门航空公司	Xiamen Airlines	MF	CXA
山东航空公司	Shandong Airlines	SC	CDG
上海航空公司	Shanghai Airlines	FM	CSF
深圳航空公司	Shenzhen Airlines	4G	CSJ
中国新华航空公司	China Xinhua Airlines	X2	CXH
云南航空公司	Yunnan Airlines	3Q	CYH
新疆航空公司	Xinjiang Airlines	XO	CXJ
四川航空公司	Sichuan Airlines	3U	CSC
武汉航空公司	Wuhan Airlines	WU	CWU
贵州航空公司	Guizhou Airlines	G4	CGH
海南航空公司	Hainan Airlines	H4	CHH
福建航空公司	Fujian Airlines	FJ	CFJ
港龙航空公司	Dragon Air	KA	KDA
大韩航空公司	Korean Air	KE	AKA
韩亚航空公司	Asiana Airlines	OZ	AAR
日本航空公司	Japan Airlines	JL	JAL
全日空公司	All Nippon Airways	NH	ANA
新加坡航空公司	Singapore Airlines	SQ	SIA
泰国国际航空公司	Thai Airways International	TG	THA
美国西北航空公司	Northwest Airlines	NW	NWA
加拿大国际航空公司	Canadian Airlines International	AC	

续表

中文名称	英文名称	2位代码	3位代码
美国联合航空公司	United Airlines	UA	UAL
英国航空公司	British Airways	BA	BAW
荷兰皇家航空公司	KLM Royal Dutch Airlines	KL	
德国汉莎航空公司	Lufthansa German Airlines	LH	DLH
法国航空公司	Air France	AF	AFR
瑞士航空公司	Swissair	SR	SWR
奥地利航空公司	Austrian Airlines	OS	AUA
俄罗斯国际航空公司	Aeroflot Russian International	SU	AFL
澳洲航空公司	Qantas Airways	QF	QFA
芬兰航空公司	Finnair Airlines	AY	FIN
意大利航空公司	Italia Airlines	AZ	AZA
斯堪的纳维亚航空公司	Scandinavian Airlines	SK	SAS
文莱皇家航空公司	Royal Brunei Airlines	BI	RBA
印度尼西亚鹰航空公司	Garuda Indonesia Airlines	GA	GIA
新加坡胜安航空公司	Singapore Silk Air	MI	MMP
马来西亚航空公司	Malaysian Airlines	MH	MAS
埃塞俄比亚航空公司	Ethiopian Airlines	ET	RTH
美国长青国际航空公司	Evergeen Int Airlines	EZ	EIA
波兰航空公司	Lot-Polish Airlines	LO	LOT
罗马尼亚航空公司	Torom Romanian Air Transport	RO	ROT
乌兹别克斯坦航空公司	Uzbekistan Airlines	HY	UZB
伏尔加第聂伯航空公司	Volga-Dnepr Airlines	VI	VDA
乌克兰航空公司	Air Ukraine	VV	UKR
哈萨克斯坦航空公司	Kazakhstan Airlines	K4	KXA
蒙古航空公司	MIAT Mongolian Airlines	OM	MGL
巴基斯坦国际航空公司	Pakistan International Airlines	PK	PIA
菲律宾航空公司	Philippine Airlines	PR	PAL
尼泊尔皇家航空公司	Royal Nepal Airlines	RA	RNA
伊朗航空公司	Iran Air	IR	IRA
朝鲜航空公司	Air Koryo	JS	KOR
以色列航空公司	Ei Ai Israel Airlines	LY	ELY
澳门航空公司	Air Macau	NX	AMU
缅甸国际航空公司	Myanmar Airways	UB	UBA
越南航空公司	Vietnam Airlines	VN	HVN

Appendix 3　附录3

Airlines' Telephone

航空公司	热线电话
中国国际航空公司	（86-010）64663366
中国南方航空（集团）公司	（86-020）86120000
中国东方航空集团公司	（86-021）62686268
深圳航空公司	（86-0755）7771999
厦门航空有限公司	（86-0592）5739888
海南航空股份有限公司	（86-0898）6798829
山东航空股份有限公司	（86-0531）8730777
四川航空公司	（86-028）5551161
法国航空公司	（86-010）65884266
英国航空公司	（86-010）65124070
加拿大航空公司	（86-010）64682001
国泰航空公司	（86-10）84868532
港龙航空公司	（86-010）65182533
日本航空公司	（86-010）65130888
大韩航空	（86-010）84538137
汉莎航空公司	（86-010）64654488
马来西亚航空公司	（86-010）65052681
西北航空公司	（86-010）65053505
澳大利亚航空公司	（86-010）64673337
北欧航空公司	（86-010）85276100
新加坡航空公司	（86-010）65052233
瑞士航空公司	（86-010）65123555
泰国航空公司	（86-010）64608899
美国联合航空公司	（86-010）64598855

References 参考文献

[1] 林扬. 民航乘务英语会话. 北京：旅游教育出版社，2017.
[2] 林扬，余明洋. 民航乘务英语视听. 北京：旅游教育出版社，2017.
[3] 黎富玉. 民航空乘英语. 北京：北京大学出版社，2015.
[4] 陆平. 民航英语口语教程. 北京：中国民航出版社，2005.
[5] 高锋. 航空乘务英语教程. 上海：同济大学出版社，2013.
[6] 黄华. 民航客舱服务实用英语. 天津：天津大学出版社，2010.
[7] 何丽娜. 实用空乘英语. 江西：江西高校出版社，2013.